PASCAGOULA DECOYS

A drake pintail with the straight line, Animal Trap Company of Miss., Inc., Pascagoula, Miss. *stamp on the bottom. This decoy is similar to the first stamped duck I saw in an antiques store in Slidell.*

PASCAGOULA DECOYS

JOE BOSCO

PELICAN PUBLISHING COMPANY
Gretna 2003

*The word "Pelican" and the depiction of a pelican are trademarks
of Pelican Publishing Company, Inc., and are registered
in the U.S. Patent and Trademark Office.*

Library of Congress Cataloging-in-Publication Data

Bosco, Joe.
  Pascagoula decoys / Joe Bosco.
      p. cm.
Includes bibliographical references.
  ISBN 1-58980-143-1 (alk. paper)
  1. Decoys (Hunting)—Mississippi—Pascagoula—Design and construction—
History. I. Title.
  SK335 .B67 2003
  745.593'6'0976212—dc21
                                        2003008558

Printed in Singapore

Published by Pelican Publishing Company, Inc.
1000 Burmaster Street, Gretna, Louisiana 70053

To my lovely wife, Susan, whose patience and encouragement made this book a reality!

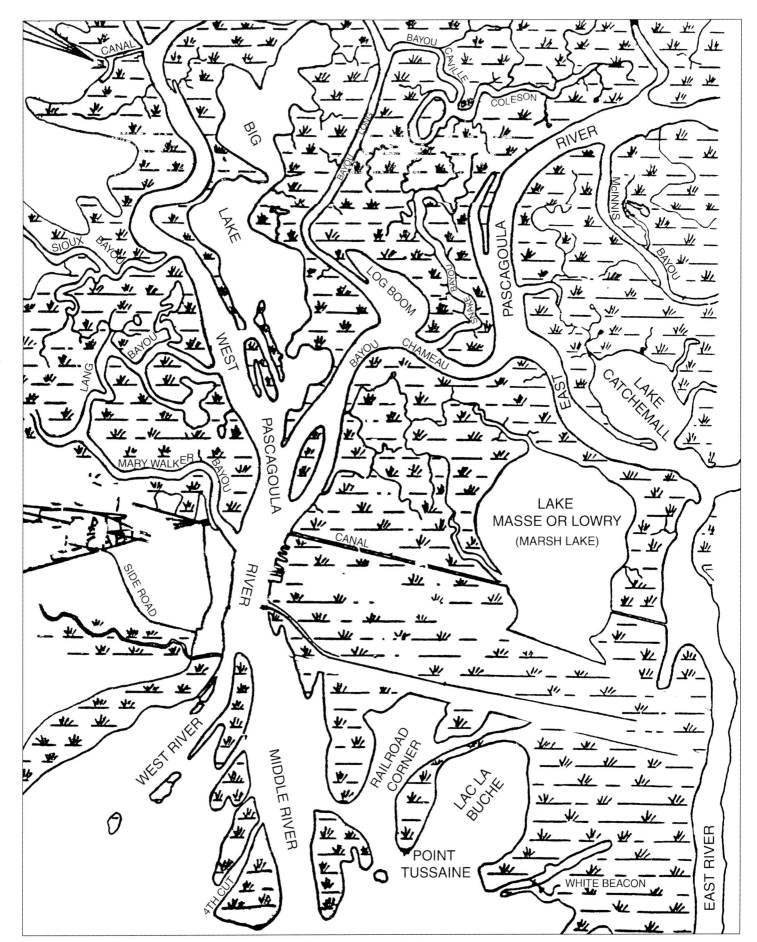

Lower Pascagoula River

CONTENTS

ACKNOWLEDGMENTS

I would like to thank all the wonderful people of Pascagoula and Jackson County, Mississippi whose cooperation and contributions made this book a reality: Jim Pelham, Louie Gasaway, Eddie Barton, Mike Torjusen, Virginia O'Sullivan, Sean O'Sullivan, Robbie O'Sullivan, Phyllis Devers, Jewel and Lucy Slade, Dena McKee, the Charles Ford family, Robert Hanning, Joe and Donna Tonelli, Chad Daggett, Tommy Wixon, Lucille Wilson, Larry and Linda Stringer, the late Dr. Perry Thompson, Elsa Martin, Lum Cumbest, Halsey Cumbest, Stewart Ramsay, John Bosco, the Jackson County Archives, and the Pascagoula Library. Without their tremendous assistance, the history of the decoy companies of Pascagoula may never have been published.

Many of these contributors are either relatives or close friends of the operators of the decoy factories that resided in this great city. For instance, the O'Sullivan family is related to the Poitevin brothers, Ellwood and Eugene. Lum Cumbest is the son of the late Roy O. Cumbest, founder of Cumbest Manufacturing Company, and was a personal friend of Frank L. Hudson. Lucille Wilson's father and brother, Emp and Elba, founded the Trehern Decoy Factory; the trio previously worked for the Hudson Manufacturing Company in the 1930s. Eddie Barton is the son of Adie Pittman; she was the second owner of the Pascagoula Decoy Company. Lucy Slade is Adie Pittman's sister and was a decoy painter for the Pascagoula Decoy Company for five years. Louie Gasaway was once employed by the Animal Trap Company of Mississippi. What better sources can an author have for the true history and facts than the actual family members and friends who were a significant part of this unique history of Pascagoula?

The other contributors are either sportsmen who purchased these fine decoys during their waterfowling years or historians knowledgeable about Pascagoula.

I would also like to thank my wife, Susan, and our longtime friend Lisa Monti, who performed proofreading and editing services.

And finally, I would be totally ungrateful if I did not offer my heartfelt thanks to the wonderful Lois Castigiolia and Betty Rodgers with the Jackson County Archives for their persistent effort in searching for articles and providing valuable research tips that made this endeavor much easier than I ever imagined.

A hen bluebill carved by my grandfather Daniel ("Ram") Van Court. This little decoy inspired my interest in decoy collecting.

INTRODUCTION

Several publications have included information about the duck decoy factories of Pascagoula, Mississippi, but *Pascagoula Decoys* is the first book exclusively dedicated to the history of the decoy companies once in operation in my hometown.

Three incidents in my life established my interest in decoy collecting. As a boy, I received a handmade bluebill decoy, one of several carved by my grandfather Daniel ("Ram") Van Court, from Ocean Springs, Mississippi. The primitive hen was made of native wood with drilled holes and weights on the bottom. I still have that decoy today. Then, as a young adult, I was following my wife, Susan, around antiques stores in Slidell, Louisiana, when I noticed a large wooden Herters Canada goose decoy. Struck by its realistic beauty, I had to own it, even though it cost me nearly a week's salary. And finally, in another antiques store, I was examining a decoy when I discovered the "Animal Trap Co. of Miss., Inc., Pascagoula, Miss." stamp on the bottom. The realization that this old decoy was made in my hometown solidified my interest in collecting wooden waterfowl decoys, those exclusively made in Pascagoula. This interest has led to many years of collecting enjoyment, browsing through antiques stores and flea markets and participating in cutthroat bidding on Ebay.

As a collector, I wanted the knowledge necessary to make good purchases, so I began to research decoys and the companies that produced them. I found that there was very little information compiled about the Pascagoula factories, and I began to make some historical notes. I started uncovering more and more fascinating information, which I then decided to compile into a book. I gathered articles and advertisements from old local newspapers, magazines, catalogs, and other decoy reference books. But the most specific and valuable information was obtained by interviewing the families and employees who were associated with these operations.

Reminiscing with some of the old-timers about duck hunting and decoy making in Pascagoula made me feel like part of this rich era, and I knew this history needed to be preserved for future generations to enjoy and appreciate. My purpose in writing this book is to document the historical facts about the Pascagoula factory decoy companies and the nationwide impact they had on the sporting industry. My hope is that *Pascagoula Decoys* will become the definitive history of the decoy companies that were located in this small South Mississippi community.

Countless hours of extensive research have gone into preparing *Pascagoula Decoys*; however, undoubtedly new information will surface. Further information about the Pascagoula companies that is forwarded to the author will be considered for inclusion in a possible revision to this book.

Two hunters using Pascagoula Decoy Company products (skiff, decoys, and paddles) during a duck hunt on the West Pascagoula River in the 1950s.

PASCAGOULA DECOYS

PASCAGOULA DECOYS

Pascagoula Decoy Company employees operating the duplicating lathe machines. A guiding arm traced the master mold, which controlled the shape of the decoy. Note the piles of sawdust.

CHAPTER 1

COLLECTING DECOYS

The evolution of duck decoys can be traced back to primitive days when American Indians used their resourceful talents to construct wild-duck decoys from a combination of mud, grass or reeds, and feathers. Hoping to get a shot with his wooden bow and arrow, the hunter arranged the fake ducks in different patterns to lure the birds within comfortable shooting range—preferably on the water. Using decoys during a hunt remains popular today.

In the late 1890s, the popularity of duck hunting increased dramatically with the advent of market hunters, or commercial hunters. Because the duck and goose populations were very strong, the commercial market was profitable, and there was a greater need for decoys. The individual hand-carvers could not keep up with demand, so this need was met by factories using duplicating lathe machines.

These machines made it possible to manufacture thousands of wooden duck decoys commercially. Up to twelve birds could be produced at the same time. The heads were drilled and fitted for glass eyes and glued for added strength. The head and body were made separate from one another and attached by a wooden dowel. Some of the heads were mounted in a fixed position while others were adjustable, allowing for different poses such as preening or sleeping.

The large numbers of birds produced by the lathe machines far surpassed the number of hand-carved decoys that were previously being produced. Nationwide, companies such as Dodge, Mason, and Stevens evolved in the late 1800s and were quickly followed by many more companies in the early 1900s.

Around 1915, the prairie pothole regions in Canada, the top duck-breeding territory, experienced severe drought that adversely affected the waterfowl population. Duck numbers were plummeting and waterfowl conservation became necessary. Then, the Migratory Bird Treaty Act of 1918 that outlawed market hunting was passed. This dealt a devastating blow to the factory decoy companies. Demand for decoys dramatically diminished to levels not seen before by these companies. Many of the smaller and family-owned businesses quickly went bankrupt and closed.

A Pascagoula goose decoy made by either the Animal Trap Company, Trehern, or Hudson Manufacturing Company. These companies advertised making lathe-turned wooden goose decoys during their production years.

By the late 1920s, the waterfowl population was flourishing again, thanks in part to Mother Nature bringing much-needed rain and snow to the Canadian prairie lands. The resurgence brought about another wave of factory decoy companies. They, and the existing factory decoy companies, continued to produce wooden decoys until the late 1950s and early 1960s, when papier-mâché and plastic models hit the market.

The Pascagoula decoy companies made a significant contribution to the rich heritage of wooden decoy production. Charles W. Grubbs, a talented whittler and hand-carver of duck calls and decoys, established the first decoy factory in Pascagoula in 1920 on the East Bank of the Pascagoula River. Frank L. Hudson purchased Grubbs' business in 1925, and the Hudson Manufacturing Company designed its own decoy, which Hudson patented. Around 1941, the company and decoy patent were sold to the Cumbest Manufacturing Company.

Up the Pascagoula River, a second decoy facility was in operation off Lake Avenue. An old family name in Pascagoula and once a dominant player in the shipbuilding industry, the Poitevin brothers, Ellwood and Eugene, had entered the duck decoy business in 1926 and sold their decoys under the brand name Singing River Decoys.

Even farther up the Pascagoula River, a third duck decoy factory began operation. Lester C. Winterton and Clifford L. Dees founded the

Pascagoula Decoy Company (PADCO) in June 1940. This company manufactured and sold duck decoys and other wooden products nationwide.

The Pascagoula area gained national recognition when the Animal Trap Company of America in Lititz, Pennsylvania—the nation's largest maker of mouse and rodent traps—purchased the Poitevin brothers' decoy operation in 1940. Around 1945, Animal Trap also purchased the Cumbest Manufacturing Company, which was previously the Hudson Manufacturing Company.

There were myriad advantages for decoy companies locating in Pascagoula. For one, decoys were made of native hardwoods such as tupelo gum and pop ash—light, buoyant, and soft woods ideal for carving—that were, and still are, extremely abundant along the Pascagoula and Escatawpa rivers.

The term "pop" described the large section of the ash tree that is cork-like, spongy, and very conducive to decoy making. The top portion of the tree was harder and heavier and offered very little value in decoy production. The tupelo gum, *Nyssa aquatica,* is recognized by its buttressed base and long, clear trunk, which opens into a narrow crown. Its range is in the southeastern United States, from Virginia south to north Florida,

A great view inside the plant of the Pascagoula Decoy Company. The blocks of wood pictured are native pop ash and tupelo gum.

A tupelo gum tree in Buzzard Lake off the Pascagoula River. Note the buttressed base of the tree.

west to southeastern Texas, and following the Mississippi River valley to south Illinois. Typically, the tree reaches eighty to ninety feet and about six to seven feet around. It has shiny leaves and blooms from March to April. The dark-purple fruit ripens in October and is devoured by wood ducks, deer, turkeys, squirrels, raccoons, and other swamp animals. A tupelo gum swamp is a magical, mysterious place appreciated by hunters and environmentalists throughout the South.

The city of Pascagoula also offered a plentiful labor force. Workers easily adapted to producing wood decoys because of their experience in the shipbuilding and sawmill industries prevalent in the area. And a third advantage for the decoy companies was the river. The companies used wood from the swamps, which could be transported to the factories by barge, greatly reducing transportation costs.

Pascagoula's decoy history spanned more than fifty years, ranging from 1920 to 1971, and all of the local decoy companies had two qualities in common—superior decoys and success! The Pascagoula companies were leaders in decoy production throughout the United States and sold their products worldwide.

The prices old wooden decoys bring today make it highly unlikely they will ever see the water again. While a hunter in the 1940s would have paid $6 to $25 per dozen for wooden decoys, a Pascagoula decoy today can fetch between $75 and $300, depending on its condition and species, and the value continues to increase. Today, these decoys are becoming harder to find for the collector.

Because the mallard was the most common bird produced, its worth is significantly lower than a rare teal or widgeon decoy. This does not mean that greenheads are cheap! If you can find one, its price range is $75 to $125. These antique birds represent a very important piece of history, especially to those who relied on this industry for their livelihood.

Thousands of duck decoys were produced and distributed by Pascagoula decoy companies, and as a result, there are still decoys to be found in antiques stores and flea markets in states as far reaching as Florida, California, and New York. Because so many of these decoys were sold nationwide to jobbers, wholesalers, and retailers, some collectors claim they are not as valuable today as other factory decoys, such as Mason or Pratt. However, many collectors, including myself, will dispute this claim after pricing an Animal Trap teal or PADCO widgeon in mint condition. It is important to remember that the history behind the factory decoy companies in the United States would not have been as rich or complete without the workmanship and production of the Pascagoula companies. Today, these decoys are receiving the attention and appreciation of collectors that they truly deserve.

A characteristic that distinguishes a Pascagoula decoy from others is the rough marks encircling the bird left by the duplicating lathe machine. These marks give the appearance of feathers, thus creating a more realistic decoy. Most competitors' birds featured a smooth finish.

The two major categories of decoys highly sought after by collectors

A PADCO mallard (top) and Animal Trap mallard (bottom). Note the difference between the two companies' work in the wing spectrum paint patterns and the lathe marks.

Drake pintails, Animal Trap (top) and PADCO (bottom).

today are hand-carved and factory-produced decoys. Renowned carvers such as Ira Hudson, Elmer Crowell, Mark Whipple, and Nicol Vidacovitch produced hand-carved decoys. These birds were primarily made in the late 1800s and early 1900s and are very expensive and difficult to find today. The factory companies played as important a role in decoy production as their predecessors, and they are just as collectible. Some of the better-known factory decoy companies included:

- Dodge, founded by Jasper Dodge around 1885 and located in Detroit, Michigan.
- Stevens, established by Harvey Stevens in Weedsport, New York around 1890.
- Mason Decoy Factory, located in Detroit, Michigan. The company began business around 1895. Mason's decoys are probably the most famous and valuable factory decoys today!
- Evans Decoy Company, founded by Walter Evans in Wisconsin in 1921.
- Herters, Inc., located in Waseca, Minnesota and still producing high-quality plastic decoys today. Their most sought-after decoys are the Canada geese, wooden owls, and crows.
- Pratt Manufacturing, founded by William E. Pratt in Joliet, Illinois around 1920.
- Animal Trap Company of America, located in Lititz, Pennsylvania. They initially made mouse and other fur-bearing-animal traps. They entered the decoy business with the purchase of Pratt in 1939. Today, they operate under the name Woodstream Corporation.
- Wildfowler Decoys, Inc., started business in 1939 in Old Saybrook, Connecticut.

There are several approaches to collecting decoys. You might pursue those produced by a particular carver or factory, or maybe decoys made in your area. I prefer the latter; my collection consists exclusively of decoys made by the Pascagoula companies. Some collectors pursue particular species such as pintails or diving ducks.

Collecting waterfowl decoys has been a passion for decades, and the number of collectors has grown significantly over the last few years. This is apparent by the numbers of decoys sold on the on-line auction giant, Ebay. Decoys are auctioned and sold throughout the world on a daily basis. They are also becoming more difficult to find in antiques stores. This increase in popularity has resulted in higher prices for collectors and investors.

While conducting interviews during my research, countless times I heard the statement, "If I only knew then what these decoys would be worth today." Many decoys were lost during a hunt, and some hunters would use the worn or damaged blocks as firewood. During the off-season, the wooden decoys were often haplessly stored in sheds and many were destroyed by termites.

There are a variety of sources available to collectors hoping to find Pascagoula decoys. One method for buying or just "screen shopping" is on-line, particularly at Internet auction sites, such as Ebay.

Ebay (www.ebay.com) is the most common on-line auction site. Practically anything can be found on this popular Web site, from antiques to magazines to jewelry to toys. Old and unique duck decoys are also available. However, although Ebay is a reputable site, new collectors should learn a few safeguards before bidding. First, educate yourself on the particular decoy you are seeking. If your interest is in PADCO decoys, become familiar with the species produced, paint and body styles, and markings. Some sellers incorrectly advertise a decoy as a particular brand or species simply from lack of knowledge on the subject. However, if you know your product, you will be able to identify a decoy accurately.

Antiques stores are another worthy source. Every time my wife and I travel, we visit stores along the route to our final destination. In fact, I purchased my first Animal Trap Company of Mississippi black mallard decoy from a dealer in southwest Georgia. He was not particularly knowledgeable (he had it advertised as a blue-winged teal), but after negotiating back and forth, I finally added it to my collection.

Another fortunate find occurred on our annual family vacation to south Florida. At one store, I located two PADCO coot decoys that were priced at only $25 each. Obviously, the owner did not recognize the true value of the PADCO coot since collectors have paid more than $200 today! I purchased both, which are pictured in this book. The next day, I found a drake mallard decoy made by the Hudson Manufacturing Company circa 1930. This rare bird was a DUO-STA model. The body pattern and paint were the typical "Pascagoula style," featuring the lathe marks left on the bird from the duplicating machine. The only distinguishing characteristics that identified the bird as a Hudson were the DUO-STA markings, which are two large, machine-drilled holes starting from the tail and going toward the head. These holes enabled the bird to float with ultimate buoyancy without the need for weights.

Estate sales provide good buying opportunities and are often advertised in the newspapers. You may also consider working with a reputable antiques dealer to serve as a contact in searching for that special decoy for your collection.

Decoy collecting can be a fun and fulfilling hobby. The true worth of a decoy is the value placed on it by the collector. For instance, the rough, handmade bluebill hen decoy made by my grandfather, which he used during his lifetime of hunting, is invaluable to me. The monetary value determined by another collector could never exceed the sentimental value of that bird!

Rare coot or poule-d'eau decoys by PADCO circa 1950s. Hunters often added a few coots to their spread as "confidence decoys" to give the impression of a safe environment to approaching birds. Not many coots were produced, thus significantly increasing their value today.

CHAPTER 2

TIMELINE OF PASCAGOULA DECOY COMPANIES

- 1868—Charles W. Grubbs markets the first commercial duck call in Illinois.
- August 15, 1888—Ellwood Cowan Poitevin born.
- 1896—Animal Trap Company founded in Abingdon, Illinois.
- 1916—Grubbs moves to Pascagoula, Mississippi.
- 1920—Grubbs establishes the first decoy factory in Pascagoula.
- 1924—Animal Trap Company name changed to Animal Trap Company of America.
- November 15, 1925—Frank Lloyd Hudson purchases the Grubbs Manufacturing Company.
- March 11, 1926—Poitevin Brothers board votes to start producing wooden duck decoys. Charles W. Grubbs is later elected company secretary.
- December 20, 1926—Grubbs departs Poitevin and eventually reestablishes his business in Houston, Texas.
- February 1928—Grubbs Manufacturing Company is renamed Hudson Manufacturing Company.
- April 9, 1929—Hudson patents his vacuum-stabilized decoys.
- 1929—Great Depression.
- August 18, 1933—Charles W. Grubbs dies.
- 1939—Animal Trap Company of America purchases the Pratt Manufacturing Company in Joliet, Illinois and starts producing lathe-turned wooden duck decoys under the brand name Victor.
- 1939-45—World War II.
- February 1940—Animal Trap Company of America purchases the Poitevin Brothers' decoy business, naming it Animal Trap Company of Mississippi.
- June 1940—Lester C. Winterton founds the Pascagoula Decoy Company.
- August 1, 1940—Fire destroys the Hudson Manufacturing Company plant off Canty Street on the Pascagoula River East Bank.

- 1941—Roy O. Cumbest purchases the Hudson Manufacturing Company, relocates the business to Wade, Mississippi, and operates under the name Cumbest Manufacturing Company.
- 1945—Animal Trap Company of America purchases Cumbest (Hudson) Manufacturing Company.
- January 3, 1946—Fire destroys the Animal Trap plant in the Poitevin building on Lake Avenue.
- 1946—Animal Trap Company relocates to Telephone Road in the old airport hangar. Ellwood Poitevin retires and Charles Weaver becomes manager. Advent of papier-mâché decoys at the Animal Trap Company.
- October 1948—Fire at the Pascagoula Decoy Company plant on North Pascagoula Street temporarily halts decoy production.
- August 17, 1951—Frank Lloyd Hudson dies.
- 1952—Tenite decoys introduced by the Animal Trap Company.
- August 14, 1952—Winterton sells property to the Pavco Veneer Mill and relocates the Pascagoula Decoy Company to 425 North Magnolia Street on the Pascagoula River.
- April 1, 1957—Adie Pittman purchases the Pascagoula Decoy Company from Winterton.
- 1959—Last year that Pascagoula Decoy Company operates at 425 North Magnolia Street and produces wooden duck decoys.
- 1960—Pascagoula Decoy Company name changes to Singing River Decoy Company and operates at 4702 North Pascagoula Street. Singing River Decoy Company starts making Styrofoam decoys and sells fishing supplies.
- 1962—Wooden decoy production ends at the Animal Trap Company of Mississippi.
- July 16, 1963—Lester C. Winterton dies.
- 1966—Animal Trap Company operates under the new parent name Woodstream Corporation.
- 1971—Singing River Decoy Company closes.
- 1971—Woodstream Corporation closes the Pascagoula plant.

Pascagoula Decoy Company Successions

| Grubbs Manufacturing Company |
(1920-25)

purchased by

| Hudson Manufacturing Company |
(1925-41)

purchased by

| Cumbest Manufacturing Company |
(1941-45)

purchased by

| Animal Trap Company |

(1940-66)

name changed to

| Woodstream Corporation |

(1966-71)

Closed 1971

| Poitevin Brothers, Inc. |

(1926-40)

purchased by

| Animal Trap Company |

(1940-66)

name changed to

| Animal Trap Company of Mississippi |

(1940-66)

name changed to

| Woodstream Corporation |

(1966-71)

Closed 1971

| Pascagoula Decoy Company |

(1940-59)

name changed to

| Singing River Decoy Company |

(1960-71)

Closed 1971

CHAPTER 3

GRUBBS MANUFACTURING COMPANY

The Grubbs Manufacturing Company was the first decoy-producing outfit in Pascagoula and one of the earlier ones in the country.

Charles W. Grubbs was born on June 25, 1848, in Clinton County, Ohio, and his family moved to Illinois while he was still a young man. In 1872, Grubbs married Amanda Hawkins and established a home on the shore of Lake Senachwine, where he began fishing commercially. In 1880, he opened the Undercliff Hotel, where he offered rooms, boat and fishing-equipment rentals, and a refreshment stand with food and tobacco products. During the spring and fall waterfowl migrations, Grubbs also offered a waterfowl-hunting guide service on the lake. His enterprises kept him busy year round.

Grubbs' successful operation did not go unnoticed. In 1882, investors constructed a new hotel with similar amenities and guide services. It is believed this had an adverse effect on Grubbs' business that resulted in his losing control of his resort. He moved to Chicago.

According to his own catalog, Grubbs made the first commercial duck call in 1868. Most historians attribute the first metal-banded, wooden-barreled duck call to Grubbs. One of the earliest ads for a Grubbs call was found in the 1889-90 Montgomery Ward catalog. Several different styles of calls were produced by Grubbs: Illinois River Duck Call, Improved Illinois River Duck Call, Kankakee Marsh Duck Call, Kankakee Crow Call, and the Miller's Improved Duck Call. These calls were made of mahogany, oak, and cedar and were sold through various sporting-goods companies and by Grubbs himself.

Grubbs came to Pascagoula in 1916 and continued making duck calls. He developed an additional interest in making wooden waterfowl decoys. In 1920, along with copartners Dr. William F. Martin and Robert Reinecke, he started producing wooden duck decoys under the name Grubbs Manufacturing Company. Grubbs literally started his decoy business with only a pocketknife and a few other hand tools, including several handsaws, files, and a hatchet. According to an article in the *Mississippi Chronicle-Star,* he hand-carved a duck decoy from pop ash wood and submitted the

First decoy factory in Pascagoula – Grubbs Manufacturing Company, 1920. From left to right: Charles W. Grubbs, owner; Eddie Bang; and son, Ernest Bang.

sample to a sporting-goods distributor. The result was an immediate order for a large quantity of decoys, and a business was born.

Grubbs set up a small factory on the Pascagoula River and soon had nationwide distribution. Later, he relocated to a larger facility off Canty Street on the banks of the Pascagoula River. A large warehouse at the Northrop Grumman Ingalls East Bank Shipyard is located there today.

Grubbs was truly a consummate wildlife artist. According to an article in the *Mississippi Chronicle-Star*, the decoys looked so natural that they could hardly be distinguished from a live duck only a few feet away. His decoys took first place at the annual Wild Fowl Decoy Exhibition held in Bellport, New York, in 1924 and the Boston Sporting Goods Show in 1925.

The demand for Grubbs' decoys increased so dramatically that additional machinery was installed at the factory. On May 16, 1922, Grubbs borrowed $1,000 from the Pascagoula National Bank and installed a patternmaker's lathe, a five-horsepower motor, a band and table saw, two twenty-eight-inch saws, a sanding machine, and other equipment to accommodate production. Hand-operated lathe machines made it possible to significantly increase output of decoys without compromising quality. As a result, Grubbs was able to meet the growing demand and he began selling decoys throughout the United States.

With the new machinery, Grubbs could produce up to 40 dozen decoys a day. He shipped 476 dozen to a wholesale company in San Francisco to meet the hunters' demand in the Pacific. Wholesale companies such as Sears Roebuck & Company, Butler Brothers, and Montgomery Ward sold Grubbs' decoys and calls across the country. Different species were sent to different regions of the country. Pacific Coast hunters demanded mallards, teal, and pintails, while the East Coast favored black mallards and diving ducks, such as bluebills, redheads, and canvasbacks. Decoy distribution began to grow across the continent. Grubbs' major markets included Bangor, Maine; Jacksonville, Florida; St. Louis, Missouri; St. Paul, Minnesota; Denver, Colorado; California; Oregon; Seattle, Washington; and Vancouver, Canada. He even shipped a dozen widgeon and mallard decoys to Zurich, Switzerland.

The species Grubbs produced were teal, mallard, black mallard, bluebill, widgeon, redhead, canvasback, pintail, and coot, and they were available in two grades. The No. 1 Perfection grade was his premier, consisting of birds made of softer woods such as pop ash and tupelo gum, with glass eyes. The selling price was $15 per dozen. The No. 2 Perfection grade was identical to No. 1 except a harder wood was utilized, and the finish was a little rougher. The selling price was $12 per dozen. Grubbs not only wanted to attract new customers, he wanted to keep his existing clients, so he offered a decoy repair service and performed sanding, repainting and restoration, glass eye replacement, and head reconstruction and refurbishment.

Drake redhead circa 1920s, Grubbs Manufacturing Company. (Collection of Joe and Donna Tonelli)

In 1924, Grubbs installed additional machinery to manufacture grass blinds, hunting coats, and other camouflage paraphernalia. The blinds were weaved with cottonlike string and rolled up for storage and transporting. He would make special trips to the Pascagoula marsh to select top-quality native grasses used in knitting the blinds and suits. The demand for the blinds also escalated to levels not seen before.

Grubbs added machinery to produce baseball bats, which were also made from pop ash logs. These were profitable in the winter months after duck hunters purchased decoys. He also manufactured a few wooden toys, such as sailboats and canoes, from the leftover wood that otherwise would have gone to waste. These nonhunting items enabled Grubbs to operate his business year round. During this time, he employed approximately twenty-five workers.

Demand for decoys increased to a point where these workers could not keep up with the backlog of orders, and the company started to suffer. In 1925, the business was sold. The transfer of stock, equipment, and real estate was made to Dr. W. F. Martin, Messrs. Gautier and Colmer, and Frank L. Hudson. The new owners almost relocated the business to the Pascagoula Ice House but decided the current location was ideal for decoy production. The plant continued operations under the Grubbs Manufacturing Company name until February of 1928, when it was changed to Hudson Manufacturing Company.

Grubbs did not remain retired very long, nor did his talents go unrecognized. On March 11, 1926, the Poitevin Brothers, Ellwood and Eugene, asked him to join their decoy-making outfit. The Poitevins were in the shipbuilding business in Pascagoula, and after World War I, they started producing wood duck decoys. Grubbs served as Poitevin's technical advisor due to his previous experience. He added a unique scope to the Poitevin production line, especially with his duck calls. However, nine months later, on December 20, 1926, Grubbs ended his association with the Poitevins and went back into business on his own. It is unknown why Grubbs left. More information of the Grubbs/Poitevin association is covered in the chapter on Poitevin Brothers.

Two years after his departure from Poitevin, Grubbs moved his business to Houston, Texas, where he continued to manufacture waterfowl calls, decoys, and grass blinds. His catalog offered blue-winged teal, mallard, pintail, and bluebill decoys. The birds were machine-lathe produced and hand painted with glass eyes. Grubbs also offered five different types of calls in his catalog: the No. 1 Perfection Call made of mahogany and cedar woods; No. 2 Call made of black walnut; No. 3 Call made of white birch, goose and crow calls; and Three-in-One Call, which was a duck, goose, and crow combination call. The price for these calls ranged from $1.25 to $5.00 each. Today, Grubbs' earliest calls can sell in excess of $1,000. The later, standard calls sell for around $150-300.

When his operation moved to Houston, Grubbs made it clear he was on his own. He boldly stated in his catalog, "We are in NO WAY connected with any other company making decoys. WE ARE MAKING OUR PRIZE-

Poitevin Brothers, Inc., stock certificate certifying Charles W. Grubbs as the owner of fifty-one shares of the company.

WINNING DECOYS, CALLS AND GRASS BLINDS." Grubbs was clearly trying to separate his business and products from those of Poitevin Brothers.

Charles W. Grubbs pioneered one of the first industries in Pascagoula and brought national attention and recognition to the state with his decoys and duck calls. An integral part of waterfowling history in the Pascagoula area, he set the stage for other decoy-manufacturing entrepreneurs to continue the successful venture he had engaged in during his thirteen years in business. Thanks to Grubbs, the name "Pascagoula" was now synonymous with wooden decoy production. Without a doubt, Charles W. Grubbs initiated the first decoy company in Pascagoula and one of the finest in the country. He died on August 18, 1933.

C. W. GRUBBS

Winner over 16 Competitors

DUCK DECOYS, CALLS AND BLINDS

608 Gray Avenue
HOUSTON, TEXAS   11/26/28

Dr C.M.Bennett

  718 Myers Building

Springfield Ill

      Dear Sir replying to your favor of the 20th

    In regard to our Corkwood decoys Thes Decoys are made of

Wood growen in the south it is Called Corkwood on account of it's

Light Weight   It does not water log or get Heavy

  Old Style Wooden Decoys are as you say get loggy in the water

   These old decoys Weight 2 to 2 3/2 pounds each

    Our Cork wood decoy Weight 10 to 12 onces eachin Full

Size Mallard   We are the Winners over All Compeitors

    Price of Decoys per Doz $15.00 Complete with anchors

     cords and weights is $18.00

    Sample Post Paid $1.50

  I inclose our catalog   Discribing the goods I make

    Hoping that I can be of service to You

    I remain yours truly   C. W. Grubbs

November 1928 letter after Grubbs left Pascagoula for Houston, Texas.

A metal reed Kankakee Crow Call circa 1920s. Many of Grubbs' calls were sold by Sears Roebuck and Hibbard Spencer & Bartlett.

This 5¼-inch call is one of last known styles produced by Grubbs. (Collection of Joe and Donna Tonelli)

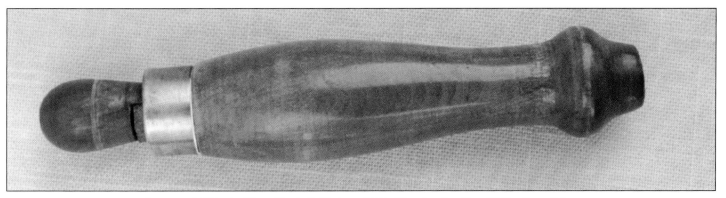

Improved Illinois River Duck Call circa 1889, Charles Grubbs. (Collection of Joe and Donna Tonelli)

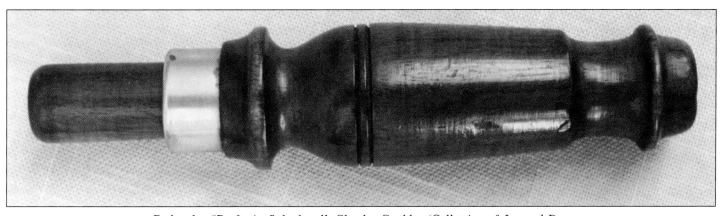

Red cedar "Perfection" duck call, Charles Grubbs. (Collection of Joe and Donna Tonelli)

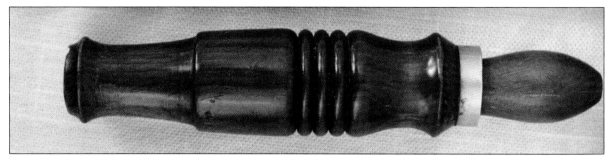

Black walnut "Presentation" duck call, Charles Grubbs. (Collection of Joe and Donna Tonelli)

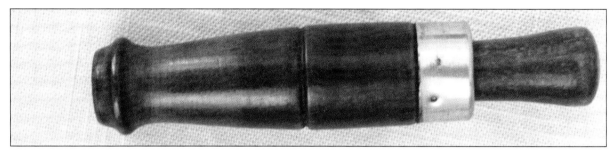

An early "Production" Grubbs duck call circa 1920s. (Collection of Joe and Donna Tonelli)

Grubbs' "Presentation" duck call made from walnut with a separate cherry mouthpiece attached to the call and a second brass ring. (Collection of Joe and Donna Tonelli)

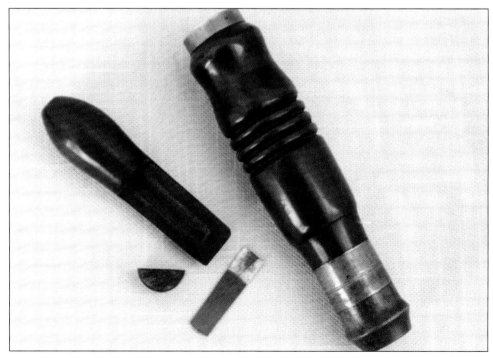

A Grubbs duck call disassembled. (Collection of Joe and Donna Tonelli)

Bird Calls.

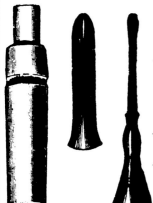

Ad from 1896-97 Montgomery Ward catalog.

A pair of mallard drake decoys circa 1920s, Grubbs Manufacturing Company.

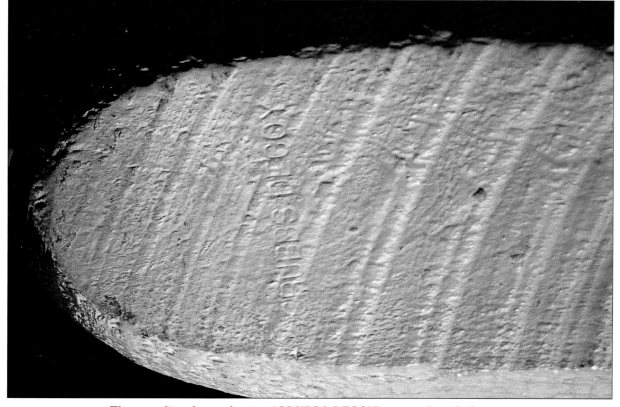

The preceding decoy, showing "GRUBBS DECOY" engraved on the bottom.

A Grubbs-style pintail drake, circa 1920s. Note the paint style that was characteristic of Grubbs' decoys.

A drake green-winged teal decoy attributed to Charles Grubbs.

Drake bluebill or scaup decoy circa 1920s, Grubbs Manufacturing Company.

Grubb's Perfection Duck Calls

The most natural calls made.
Ask the ducks.

No. 1. East Indian vermillion wood, gold mounted, silver reed, which assures the perfect tone. Postpaid, **$5.**
Black walnut call, **$2.50.**

C. W. GRUBBS   Pascagoula, Miss.

Ad from National Sportsman Magazine, *December 1920.*

True to Life Decoys

Lightest weight wood. Resists water. Feather finish. Solid. Buy from dealer or direct.
Catalog and prices on request

GRUBBS MFG. CO., Inc.
P. O. Box 146,   **Pascagoula, Miss.**
Winners of Prizes New York Exposition 1924

Ad from Hunting & Fishing Magazine, *August 1926.*

GRUBBS PERFECTION DUCK CALL

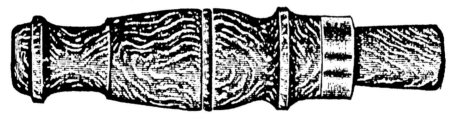

This call is made by C. W. Grubbs, who originated the first duck call in 1868, and is the result of many years' study of the habits and call of the wild duck. It is made in two grades and is the most perfect of all calls in tone and quality and is fully guaranteed.

"A" Grade is made of East Indian vermillion wood, which gives forth the purest tone, the reed is of highly tempered silver and call is gold mounted. Weight, 2 oz.
G1235 Price, each.....................................$3.00 net

"B" Grade is made of black walnut and nickel silver mounted with nickel silver reed, finely tempered, and perfect tone; weight, 2 oz.
G1236 Price, each.....................................$1.50 net

"Grubbs" Instructions, "How and When to Call Ducks," given with each call.

Ad from the 1932 Von Lengerke & Antoine catalog. This is one of the last advertisements for Grubbs' products before his death in 1933.

CHAPTER 4

HUDSON MANUFACTURING COMPANY

The Hudson Manufacturing Company was another Pascagoula decoy company that achieved national acclaim. The founder and president of the company was Frank Lloyd Hudson, who was born in 1871 in LaGrange, Troup County, Georgia, and obtained degrees from Auburn University, Georgia Tech, and Cornell University. With an intimate knowledge of mechanical and electrical engineering and chemistry, he began his construction-industry career as a supervisor at two cotton mills in Georgia and later for Troup Chemical Company. Fearing the chemical fumes might be detrimental to his health, Hudson left the company in 1911.

America's entrance into World War I brought about a change of direction for Hudson. During this time, the United States needed ships and supplies. The U.S. military recruited the few men, including Hudson, who were technically knowledgeable about engineering and shipbuilding. Officials were so impressed with Hudson that they appointed him assistant superintendent at Port Wentworth in Savannah, Georgia.

At the age of fifty-two, Hudson moved to Pascagoula, enjoying the quiet and friendliness of the charming city. Three years later, he married Katherine Perry Curry. Hudson was introduced to Charles W. Grubbs and Dr. W. F. Martin and toured the Grubbs decoy operation. He was so interested in the decoy business that he purchased the Grubbs Manufacturing Company on November 25, 1925. Hudson operated the business at the same location and under the Grubbs name until February 1928, when he changed it to Hudson Manufacturing Company.

The Hudson Manufacturing Company continued where Grubbs left off—producing and selling quality wooden decoys and duck calls throughout the country. His plant had an ideal location to accommodate this production. The building, constructed of a sheet-metal roof and sides, was located on the East Bank of the Pascagoula River on Henry Avenue off Canty Street. The administration office was located south of the main plant on the riverbank.

Hudson initially manufactured solid wooden duck decoys until 1929, when he developed the first patented decoy in the country—a vacuum-stabilized waterfowl decoy made from the butts of carefully selected pop ash and tupelo gum woods native to the area. This style enabled the decoy to ride higher on the water, eliminating the need for balance weights. It also generated a ripple effect from the wind and waves that gave the appearance of a live duck on the water. These decoys gained enormous popularity and had nationwide distribution. He even shipped his products to Canada and some European countries.

Hudson's patent was "holes" in the bottom, which improved buoyancy and made the decoys 20 to 30 percent lighter than their solid counterparts. Three different models were produced: VAC-STA, DUO-STA, and MONO-STA.

The VAC-STA decoy had two concave hollows forming two separate air pockets. This caused the decoys to ride upright and balanced on the water under varied conditions. The VAC-STA decoy was made in both a deluxe and climax model. The deluxe model was a very large, magnum-style bird with a high-grade paint and exquisite detail work. The climax model was similar to the deluxe but a little smaller. Both were made in VAC-STA and DUO-STA models and were lightweight and buoyant. The VAC-STA was, by far, Hudson's best-selling decoy.

The feature of the DUO-STA style was two round holes drilled through

A VAC-STA pintail circa 1940, Hudson Manufacturing Company.

Hudson mallards in original condition, circa 1930s.

The three patented Hudson decoys. From left to right: DUO-STA, MONO-STA, and VAC-STA.

the solid body from the tail toward the head. Air was trapped in the upper part of the body, which caused the decoy to ride high on the water. This unique feature presented a very lifelike appearance of a wild duck on the water.

The MONO-STA was Hudson's economy-priced decoy for the cost-conscious hunter. This streamlined model featured a large flat bottom with a single round hole drilled upward through the body from the tail section toward the head.

The decoys were extremely popular with hunters around the United States. National request was so high that Hudson found it a challenge to meet demand. Like other Pascagoula decoy factories, Hudson Manufacturing made these blocks from the butt of the pop ash tree, which is the portion of the tree that is submerged in the waters of the Pascagoula swamp. The duck species produced included mallard, pintail, teal, broadbill, coot, whistler, widgeon, black duck, redhead, canvasback, bluebill, blackjack, and sheldrake. Hudson also produced a few goose decoys: brant, Canada goose, and a rare blue goose. Upon special request from his clients, he made unique and unusual posing decoys. Most of these special orders were geese designed with different head positions. Salesman samples or miniatures were made in mallard, bluebill, and pintail drakes.

The Hudson Manufacturing plant expanded its offerings for the duck hunter. Besides decoys, it produced duck and goose calls, grass hunting suits, and marsh-grass duck blinds. According to an advertisement in the *Mississippi Chronicle-Star* in 1935, Hudson was the world's largest manufacturer of duck decoys, calls, grass blinds, and suits. Twelve employees were busy working overtime to fill the backlog of orders. These employees, including three women who painted and installed the glass eyes, produced up to thirty dozen decoys a day. In 1938, Hudson produced and sold more than six thousand dozen decoys nationwide.

In August of 1936, a fire started in a small building at the Hudson plant that damaged about forty-five dozen rough-cut decoys. The building housed a dry kiln machine, dozens of duck decoys, and pop ash timber used to make the decoys. The building and equipment were damaged, and Hudson estimated the loss to be approximately $125. On August 1, 1940, another fire broke out in the Hudson plant and destroyed one of the dry kilns along with hundreds of decoys. The loss was estimated in the thousands of dollars. Although the origin of the fire was never determined, Hudson speculated the cause was the kiln machine itself. According to the Pascagoula Fire Department, the blaze started around 5:00 A.M. and very little could have been done to save the building and its contents.

Fires were fairly common in decoy factories. The primary causes were workers smoking, dry kilns overheating, and a petroleum derivative chemical called naphtha. Naphtha was mixed with paint and used as a drying agent to speed the process. It was very flammable and volatile.

In December 1940, Ingalls Shipbuilding made an offer to purchase the Hudson Manufacturing plant and property for $1,500. The site was needed for the construction of warships for the United States Navy. Ingalls was

A rare DUO-STA hen bluebill, Hudson Manufacturing Company.

acting as an agent for the navy in negotiating a fair price for the property. The proposal took Hudson by surprise, since he was contemplating rebuilding the plant after the fire. However, he was getting older and starting to develop health problems. In January 1941, Ingalls made the purchase for $2,400. Today, a large warehouse occupies the area where Hudson's plant once stood.

Hudson's health continued to deteriorate, so he decided to sell his equipment and the patented decoys to longtime friend and business associate Roy O. Cumbest. Cumbest, who previously provided Hudson with wood for decoy making, operated the business under the name Cumbest Manufacturing Company. The decoy operation was moved to the Cumbest sawmill in Wade, Mississippi.

On August 17, 1951, Frank Lloyd Hudson died of a heart condition at the age of eighty at his home on Columbus Drive in Pascagoula.

A Hudson VAC-STA hen bluebill.

Bottom view of the patented VAC-STA decoy, Hudson Manufacturing.

A VAC-STA drake redhead decoy circa 1930s.

A VAC-STA drake redhead, Hudson Manufacturing.

A pair of Hudson VAC-STA climax mallards circa 1930s.

A Hudson VAC-STA climax bluebill.

45

A pair of Hudson DUO-STA deluxe mallards circa 1930s.

Back view showing Hudson's DUO-STA design.

A rare VAC-STA drake blue-winged teal in original condition, circa 1930s.

A pair of VAC-STA mallards in original condition, Hudson Manufacturing.

An early solid drake pintail decoy. The solid versions were made prior to 1929, when Hudson patented the VAC-STA model.

Hudson drake mallard decoy circa 1930s.

Two MONO-STA drake mallards made in the 1930s.

A Hudson deluxe drake pintail and salesman sample decoy.

49

This Hudson mallard was found under the pier of Lewis Sporting Goods, a local landmark, and repainted by Lucille Wilson.

A Hudson drake bluebill decoy in mint, original condition.

Ad from Jackson County Business Review, *1935.*

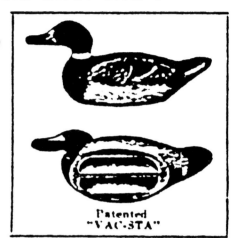
Ad from Chronicle-Star, *June 1940.*

53

In 1938, Hudson's business was advertised as one of the largest decoy manufacturers in the world.

CHAPTER 5

POITEVIN BROTHERS, INC. (SINGING RIVER DECOYS)

At an early age, Ellwood and Eugene Poitevin learned the boat-building business while employed at local shipyards in the early 1900s. They learned fundamental construction principles, and in 1905 they started their own shipyard south of the Pascagoula River Bridge, where they built ships, boats, and barges. The enterprise was named Poitevin Brothers, and another successful Pascagoula industry got its start.

In September 1906, shortly after the brothers had started their business, a hurricane struck the Pascagoula area and almost wiped them out. Their ground ways were damaged and the first boat under construction was all but sunk. However, this misfortune did not stop the Poitevins from achieving their dreams. The first boat they launched after forming the partnership was a twenty-two-foot vessel christened the *May,* because it was launched in that month of 1907. The boat was powered by a one-cylinder, six-horsepower Miami engine.

In 1916, bad luck struck again with another powerful hurricane. The storm swept through the area and damaged the Poitevin yard and boats under construction to a point where they had no choice but to relocate the business. They settled on a site at the end of Lake Avenue on the Pascagoula River.

On August 10, 1923, the Poitevin Brothers decided to incorporate their business in Pascagoula. The purpose was to buy, sell, and manufacture lumber and construct boats and barges. Poitevin stock in the amount of $25,000 was issued, and the principal owners were defined as follows: Ellwood Poitevin, president and treasurer (251 shares), Eugene Poitevin, vice-president and secretary (251 shares), and George J. Rodriguez (1 share).

In their forty years of boat building, Poitevin Brothers built everything from skiffs to 100-foot barges, Biloxi schooners to catboats. The largest sailing boats they constructed were two 72-foot schooners, the *Missala* and the *Miss Columboa*. They also built a 54-foot cruiser called the *Silver Spray.*

On March 11, 1926, a special board of directors meeting was held, and a decision was made to manufacture wooden waterfowl decoys and sell

Ellwood C. Poitevin, circa 1950s.

Circa 1930.

them under the brand name Singing River Decoys. They invited Charles W. Grubbs to join the company. Grubbs had previously established the first decoy operation in Pascagoula, and he brought great value to the Poitevin operation with both his knowledge and line of decoys, duck calls, grass hunting suits, and blinds. The board also voted to approve the purchase of equipment from Grubbs for $1,275. Grubbs was to be paid in Poitevin stock at face value; fifty-one shares were issued to Grubbs in exchange for his sporting-goods equipment. Two weeks later, the board of directors elected Grubbs as secretary of the corporation, and just a few months later, he was appointed general manager of the sporting-goods division, with an annual salary of $1,500. However, speculation had it that Grubbs and the Poitevins soon had a falling out, and only nine months later, on December 20, 1926, Grubbs transferred back his Poitevin stock in return for his inventory and machinery. He immediately turned in his resignation as secretary and Poitevin Brothers accepted. The Poitevin decoy operation continued.

Though it began as a small subsidiary enterprise of the Poitevins' boat-building business, the decoy-making segment grew to such proportions that it eclipsed their original business and became the main division. The tupelo gum and pop ash woods used in making the decoys were abundant and native along the Pascagoula River. The lightweight decoys were very popular with sportsmen across the nation, and shipments were made throughout the United States, Canada, and Mexico. Poitevin Brothers'

Pascagoula, Miss.

Poitevin's Singing River Decoys letterhead, 1928.

Singing River Decoys were marketed and sold by Sears Roebuck, Montgomery Ward, and sporting-goods stores around the country.

Poitevin Brothers produced the following species of waterfowl decoys: mallard, black duck, baldpate, teal, bluebill, redhead, canvasback, pintail, whistler, mud hen, and goose. They primarily made solid wood decoys in the following grades: perfection, mammoth, solid, and ideal. Another popular style was the "solid hollow" decoy. It had two hollowed-out or concave holes on the bottom similar to the VAC-STA decoy produced by Hudson. This design made the bird lighter and easier for the hunter to carry.

In June of 1928, the Poitevins filed an application for a decoy patent with the United States Patent Office in Washington, D.C. Under the advisement of their attorney, they filed for a patent because competitors were producing similar models. One theory claimed the competitor was Grubbs, since this time period coincided with the Grubbs-Poitevin split and Grubbs' relocation to Houston, where he started producing waterfowl decoys again. Another reason behind the patent filing may have been Hudson Manufacturing Company's VAC-STA decoy (which was patented in 1929). Poitevin produced the solid hollow version that was very similar in appearance. However, I could not find if the patent was ever granted to Poitevin or if, in fact, Grubbs or Hudson were the competitors in question.

Poitevin continued manufacturing and selling thousands of duck decoys nationwide. In 1931, demand increased to a point where they had a difficult time filling orders. Poitevin borrowed $1,000 from the Pascagoula National Bank to purchase additional equipment. As collateral, hundreds of dozens of decoys were put up along with other sporting-goods equipment. This decision enabled the company to grow, since, in 1937, the Poitevin Brothers produced over 100 dozen duck decoys each

Bluebill or scaup decoys, Poitevin Brothers.

Our Superior Decoys

Lifelike, Light and Durable

Manufactured by

Poitevin Bros., Inc.

111 Lake Avenue

PASCAGOULA, MISS.

All Solid Hollow Decoys made in Perfection Grade.

All the large species of Ducks made Solid Hollow.

All Mammoth or large decoys made Solid Hollow and in Perfection Grade.

All Geese Decoys made Solid Hollow and in Perfection Grade.

All the above made to order; only a limited amount of Perfection Grade carried in stock, as Mallard, Canvas-back, Red Heads, etc.

All Perfection Grade Decoys are carefully selected from wood that is extra light, dry, and free from all defects.

The Solid Hollow Decoys are all Perfection Grade, Hollowed out by our special method, and are solid, and not made in two sections and glued together.

All ideal Grade Decoys are those that will not take the above grade, but under no circumstances will culls be included in this grade, as they are inspected for defects, etc. as the other grades and so graded.

ALL DECOYS ARE PAINTED WITH THE SAME GRADE OF PAINT, WITH THE SAME CARE, AND THE SAME AS IN THE BEST GRADE.

TROSCLAIR PRINT. PLAQUEMINE

The 1930 company brochure (front cover and inside front cover)

week and twenty-seven people were employed in the decoy plant.

The success and quality of Poitevin's Singing River Decoys attracted national attention in February of 1940 when the Animal Trap Company of America, located in Lititz, Pennsylvania, purchased the decoy business and equipment. The acquisition gave Animal Trap a strong presence in the South and continued production of the popular Poitevin styles. Additional information on the Poitevin Brothers/Animal Trap purchase will be found in the chapter on Animal Trap Company of Mississippi.

A rough-cut Poitevin mallard decoy circa 1930s.

A supreme-grade Poitevin black duck.

A Poitevin drake bluebill.

A Poitevin ideal-grade (left) and Victor mallard (right). The Poitevin birds had a rougher finish than their successor. The Animal Trap Company continued this popular Poitevin style after the purchase in 1940, stamping its brand name "VIC- TOR" on the bottom.

A Poitevin salesman sample pintail along with the original.

A Poitevin economy-style drake bluebill.

A rare Poitevin drake blue-winged teal circa 1930s.

An ideal-grade Poitevin drake bluebill circa 1930s.

An economy model or "Ideal Jr."-grade black duck circa 1930s.

A Poitevin drake redhead decoy in original condition.

An economy-grade canvasback drake. This style had a thin profile, feather finish with original red glass eyes. This model was also known as a wing-duck or "cull" decoy.

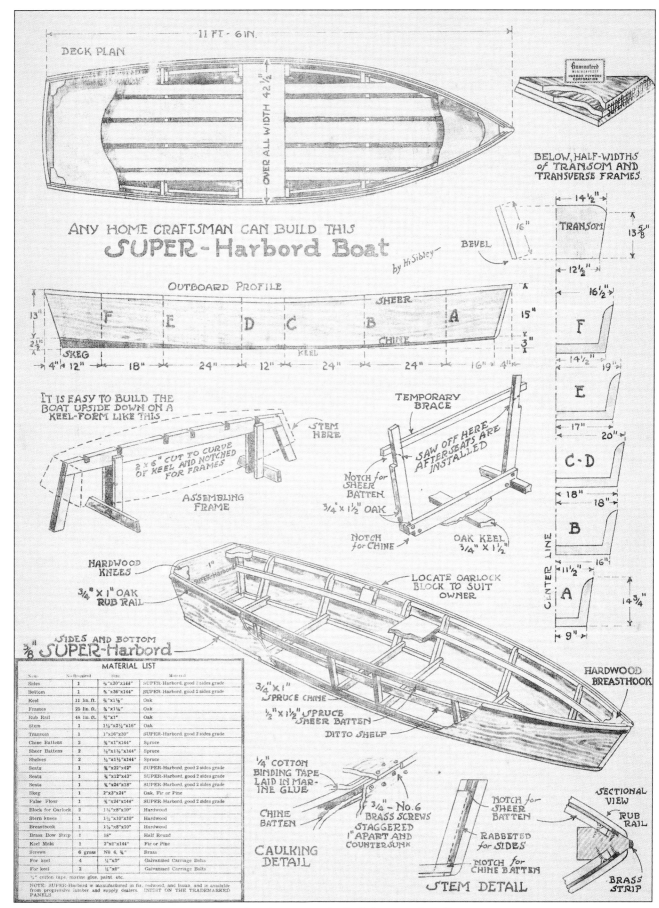

Design plans for Poitevin's duck boats and skiffs.

The Smartest Sportsmen
Say—
SINGING
RIVER
DECOYS

Our sea craft are "Bred In The Wood" to give satisfactory performance and long time service. From the smallest of skiffs to the trim smacks and yachts, Poitevin built boats are in demand.

After all is said and done a boat can only be as good as the wood and workmanship that goes into it. That's why boats by Poitevin are always given the preference.

Good decoy ducks, grass blinds, grass hunting suits and duck calls are the secret of successful hunting. Poitevin Brothers hunting outfits are better because they receive more expert attention.

Years of experience in the manufacturing of all necessary duck hunting materials have given this company a natural advantage. Consequently it isn't unusual that the wiser sportsmen ask for Poitevin Brothers products.

POITEVIN BROTHERS

BOAT BUILDERS   PASCAGOULA, MISS.

Ad from Jackson County Business Review, *July 1931.*

SINGING RIVER DECOYS

MANUFACTURED BY POITEVIN BROTHERS

MADE OF POP ASH WOOD

Pop Ash, a cork-like wood in texture and weight, from which the native inhabitants have always made hand carved decoys for their personal use, has only recently been put on the world market as a commercial decoy. Its qualities have quickly been appreciated by sportsmen everywhere. The supply is practically unlimited.

Of its native growing places, the Pascagoula River lowlands are the most famous. According to history, this river formed the boundary line of two hostile Indian camps—the Biloxi and Pascagoula tribes. They met in combat one day and rather than surrender, the remaining Pascagoula tribe retreated to its banks and disappeared under its waves, singing their war songs. Since that time faint musical tones can be heard on still nights emanating from the river ripples. Science has been baffled in seeking its source. Thousands of visitors have been amazed after hearing its famous music. It is still a mystery as deep as ever. Hence the name **SINGING RIVER DECOYS**

DECOYS AND
GAME CALLS

PRICE LIST

8 MALES, 4 FEMALES—ONE DOZEN

	Shipping Wt. 19 Lbs. **SUPERIOR DECOY** Made in all species. Hollowed out with special tools, much lighter than other decoys. Standard package quantity	Per Doz.	Per Doz.

PERFECTION DECOY

8 MALES, 4 FEMALES—ONE DOZEN

Shipping Wt. 27 lbs. Made in all species, same size and painting as Superior, made of solid block not hollowed out. Standard package quantity.

PERFECTION JR. DECOY

8 MALES, 4 FEMALES—ONE DOZEN

Shipping Wt. 20 lbs. Same artistic painting and finish as Perfection, thinner through body from center of back.

IDEAL DECOY

8 MALES, 4 FEMALES—ONE DOZEN

Shipping Wt. 27 lbs. Made in all species. Standard package quantity. All Species.

IDEAL JR. DECOY

8 MALES, 4 FEMALES—ONE DOZEN

Shipping Wt. 20 lbs. Same as above, thinner through body from center of back.

EUREKA DECOY

8 MALES, 4 FEMALES—ONE DOZEN

Shipping Wt. 15 lbs. Mallard Specie Only Standard package quantity.

ALL DECOYS FURNISHED WITH GLASS EYES

"OUR PRICES ARE AS LOW AS THE BEST
OUR DECOYS ARE BETTER THAN THE REST"

Ad from Jackson County Business Directory, *1963.*

Ad from Hunting & Fishing Magazine, *1929.*

Poitevin Brothers stock certificate for Ellwood Poitevin signed by Charles W. Grubbs, company secretary, 1926.

Elba Trehern, circa 1940s.

CHAPTER 6

TREHERN DECOY FACTORY

E. A. ("Emp") Trehern (1884-1959) and his son Elba (1907-66) initially worked for the Hudson Manufacturing Company in the 1930s. Emp operated the lathe machines used to cut the decoys; Elba was the general manager. After the 1940 fire at the Hudson Manufacturing plant, the Treherns left and started their own decoy company in Pascagoula under the name Trehern Decoy Factory. The small factory was located at the fork of Orchard Road and Old Mobile Highway in a small building constructed by Elba. While the building no longer stands, the property remains in the family today.

The company employed twelve to fifteen people. Four to five women, including Elba's wife, Pauline, painted the solid wood ducks, primarily as mallards and Canada geese. The company manufactured about fifty dozen decoys a day that were packed twelve to a box and sold for $12 per dozen. Lucille Wilson, Elba's sister, noted that the Trehern decoys were mostly sold from outside this area. She said they were shipped to mail-order houses and large sporting-goods stores in the North. "I don't recall ever seeing these ducks for sale around Pascagoula," said Wilson. "I guess they just didn't sell."

The decoys were made from the native tupelo gum trees, which are abundant along the Pascagoula and Escatawpa river swamps. Because they were made from the same wood and with no identifying marks, it is doubtful that one of these decoys can ever be accurately identified or distinguished from other Pascagoula decoys.

The Trehern Decoy Factory remained in business a very short time. On April 15, 1941, Elba Trehern decided to sell the business due to increased local competition and high labor costs. Elba sold the building, his equipment, and 556 dozen rough-cut decoy bodies to the Pascagoula Decoy Company. The new company retained him as an employee because of his experience and craftsmanship. According to the Jackson County land-deed records, the Pascagoula Decoy Company used the facility until the end of the year. Elba Trehern later died of a heart attack on August 30, 1966.

Roy O. Cumbest, circa 1956.

CHAPTER 7

CUMBEST MANUFACTURING COMPANY

Roy O. Cumbest (1903-57) entered the timber and trucking business as an independent operator in the early 1930s. He had a lumber and sawmill establishment in Wade, Mississippi that operated under the name Cumbest Manufacturing Company from 1939 to 1999. In the 1940s, the mill sold cypress wood to shipyards in Texas, Mississippi, Alabama, and Florida. Cumbest also sold ash wood to Dodge and Chrysler for use as panels on the outside of their cars.

In 1941, Cumbest purchased the Hudson Manufacturing Company, moved it to Wade, and continued to produce Hudson's patented VAC-STA decoys. It is virtually impossible to distinguish between an original Hudson decoy and one manufactured by Cumbest. The Cumbest family harvested the butts of tupelo gum and pop ash trees from Culbert, Gar, and Caswell lakes off the upper east part of the Pascagoula River swamp. Cumbest cut and floated the wood down the river to Cumbest Bluff, where it was transported to their mill and then cut into 4x8-inch sections for decoy making.

Cumbest also continued to make the popular grass blinds and hunting suits. Employees would travel the bayous between Bay St. Louis and Pascagoula harvesting tall, quality marsh grass. The grass was handwoven into blinds and shipped around the country, the primary markets being Wisconsin and Michigan. Cumbest advertised their product by sending mail-outs and letters to sporting-goods stores and by word of mouth. Sears Roebuck also carried their popular product line.

Two key employees who previously worked at the Hudson Manufacturing Company were Mack and Lucille Wilson. According to Lum Cumbest, son of the late Roy Cumbest, Lucille Wilson was an "expert decoy painter and a valuable asset to the company." She had great experience from her previous years with Hudson. Mack Wilson operated the machinery. The Wilsons had an interest in the company and, in fact, the company was almost named Cumbest-Wilson Manufacturing Company. However, the Wilsons wanted to move back to Pascagoula, so they only worked a couple more years.

The Cumbest plant had sufficient equipment to produce birds in great volume. There were five dry kilns, which dried the wood to the proper moisture content, and three duplicating lathe machines. The lathe

Cumbest Manufacturing Company, circa 1945.

machines comprised knives that followed a steel or iron reproduction pattern. According to Lum Cumbest, after the decoy heads were turned on the lathe, they were put in a barrel that was rotated by motors. The barrel would slowly turn until the heads were relatively smooth. Up to a hundred heads could be sanded at a time. Afterwards, they were hand-sanded, primed, painted, and attached to the bodies with a wooden dowel for the finished product.

Like many of the other decoy businesses, the Cumbest Manufacturing Company was severely impacted by World War II. Cumbest directed all their efforts toward the United States war campaign, providing wood for shipbuilding to the U.S. Navy. Their decoy production stopped during this time.

Cumbest considered producing wooden duck decoys after the war, but by this time, the synthetic and papier-mâché models were emerging on the market. The decoy business had become very competitive, and it was cost prohibitive to produce the birds from wood. Around 1945, Cumbest Manufacturing approached the Animal Trap Company of America to see if they were interested in purchasing their decoy business. The Animal Trap Company had previously purchased the Poitevin Brothers' decoy operation in 1940. Besides, the Animal Trap Company was equipped to produce the papier-mâché models along with their popular wooden version. The Animal Trap Company of America made the purchase and acquired their second decoy company.

Although the Hudson and Cumbest manufacturing companies ended their production of wooden duck decoys, their ever-popular patented VAC-STA model was continued by the Animal Trap Company of Mississippi and remained one of the best-selling decoys in the country through the 1950s.

The sawmill in Wade, Mississippi, 1950s.

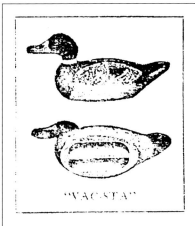

CUMBEST MANUFACTURING CO.

Manufacturers of

HUDSON'S PATENTED DECOYS

VAC-STA   MONO-STA   DUO-STA

GRASS BLINDS

Pascagoula, Miss.

Cumbest letterhead, circa 1940s.

CUMBEST MANUFACTURING CO.

MANUFACTURERS OF

HUDSON'S PATENTED DECOYS

PASCAGOULA, MISS.

"VAC-STA"

PATENTED

Cumbest stationery, circa 1940s.

CHAPTER 8

ANIMAL TRAP COMPANY
OF MISSISSIPPI

In 1896, the Animal Trap Company was established in Abingdon, Illinois, where they manufactured mouse and rat traps. They were in direct competition with the J. M. Mast Manufacturing Company of Lancaster, Pennsylvania. In 1902, the Mast factory relocated to Lititz, Pennsylvania, and their trap business grew to a point where they began to cut into the business of the Animal Trap Company. In 1905, the two businesses consolidated and operated from Lititz under the Animal Trap Company name. In 1924, under the guidance of C. M. Woolworth, president and founder of the famous Woolworth department stores, the name was changed to the Animal Trap Company of America. The company continued to manufacture mouse, rat, and other rodent traps and sold them under the brand name Victor. They produced about 90 percent of the traps sold in the country.

In 1939, the Animal Trap Company of America purchased the Pratt Manufacturing Company located in Joliet, Illinois. Pratt produced lathe-turned factory duck decoys for nineteen years, and the company and equipment were sold after the death of founder and owner William E. Pratt. The Animal Trap Company of America started the production of Victor duck decoys.

Various styles and grades of decoys were produced. The Number 1 grade was their standard size with a deluxe finish. The Number 2 model was their mammoth or magnum size produced in a premier finish. The Number 12 or economy-grade was made from the cull wood. This style was a thinner, rougher-cut decoy with deep lathe marks encircling the body and head. According to Stewart Ramsay, a lifelong Pascagoula resident and an ardent hunter, the culls could be purchased for fifty cents each back in the early 1950s. Today, however, they command anywhere from $75 to $125! This style was well made and carefully painted to true natural color but priced to match all competitors' economy models. The Number 5 goose decoys were sanded smooth with a premier finish and measured approximately seventeen inches. Animal Trap briefly continued the hollow model decoy, which was originally produced by the Pratt Manufacturing Company. These birds were bored through the breast for

No. 12 grade Victor drake pintail, circa 1940s.

Pair of Animal Trap mallards. The hen is their No. 2 magnum-size model.

No. 12 Victor drake bluebill made in the sleeping position.

lightening and then sealed with a wooden plug. It is doubtful that this model was ever made in Pascagoula since no Pascagoula advertisements or stamps have been found for any of these decoys.

The Animal Trap Company was divided into four manufacturing departments: mousetrap, steel-trap, hand garden tools, and duck decoys. Their product line included traps; Trump garden tools; hunting knives; decoys; duck, crow, and goose calls; and other hunting accessories. Their duck decoy division was the largest and most successful sector of the company.

Since trapping and waterfowl hunting were extremely popular throughout the country, the Animal Trap Company decided to establish a plant in the South to better serve the growing Southern market for traps and duck decoys. They were attracted to the quality decoys and solid reputation of the Poitevin Brothers. As a result, in February 1940, the Animal Trap Company of America purchased the Poitevin Brothers' decoy operation from Ellwood C. Poitevin, who previously purchased his brother Eugene's interest in the decoy-making part of the company. Animal Trap now had a solid foundation in the South.

It is interesting to note that in April 1939, C. M. Woolworth, president of the Animal Trap Company of America, visited Pascagoula and met with Frank L. Hudson. This was almost a year prior to their purchase of the Poitevin Brothers' decoy operation. He toured Hudson's decoy plant and was very impressed with the patented VAC-STA decoy. Was the Animal Trap Company interested in purchasing the Hudson Manufacturing Company prior to Poitevin? This question is left for speculation.

Poitevin's Singing River Decoys were sold across the United States,

Canada, Mexico, and New Zealand. With the Poitevin addition, the Animal Trap Company was on its way to becoming the largest decoy manufacturer in the country. They now had two subsidiaries: Niagara Falls, Ontario, and Pascagoula, Mississippi.

The Pascagoula plant operated under the name Animal Trap Company of Mississippi, Inc. It was, by far, the more productive and prominent subsidiary in manufacturing waterfowl decoys. The business was located at 111 Lake Avenue and operated throughout the year. The two-level building was made of heart pine with sheet-metal siding. The male employees operated the machinery on the bottom floor while the female employees painted the birds and installed the eyes in the loft. During this time, ten men and four women produced more than 3,000 decoys each week, and demand continued to grow.

VICTOR DECOYS

MADE IN

ALL SPECIES

MADE IN

ALL GRADES

| MALLARD | REDHEAD | PINTAIL | WIDGEON | CANVAS BACK |
| TEAL | BLUE BILL | WHISTLER | BLACK DUCK | MUD HEN |

Made From the Famous Light Weight

Pop Ash of Jackson County

Pop Ash Produces the Lightest Weight Commercial Decoy. All Heads and Bodies Painted True to Nature.

SOLD BY SPORTING GOODS DEALERS EVERYWHERE

ANIMAL TRAP COMPANY OF MISSISSIPPI

PASCAGOULA, MISS.

Subsidiary of Animal Trap Co. of America

Ad from Chronicle-Star, *June 1940. This is one of the first advertisements for Victor decoys after Animal Trap purchased Poitevin in 1940.*

In July of 1940, Ellwood Poitevin, the plant's manager, announced that a corporate decision was made to produce virtually all of the Animal Trap decoys at the Pascagoula plant. The tupelo gum and pop ash woods from which the Pascagoula decoys were made had been found to be lighter, more buoyant, and superior to the white pine used at the Northern plants. This decision provided an economic stimulus to Pascagoula.

In 1945, the Animal Trap Company of America made its second Southern acquisition when it purchased the Cumbest (Hudson) Manufacturing Company, which added the highly popular VAC-STA decoy to its product line. This strategic move made the Animal Trap Company an even more dominant player in the duck decoy manufacturing business.

On Thursday afternoon, January 3, 1946, a fire broke out at the Animal Trap plant in the building owned by the Poitevins. According to Virginia O'Sullivan, daughter of Ellwood Poitevin, the fire started when an employee inadvertently threw a match into a can of paint thinner. The sudden explosion quickly resulted in a fire that spread throughout the building, completely destroying the factory, decoys, and several outbuildings. The blaze started in the upstairs loft in the paint room, where the women were spray-painting the decoys. One employee reported a noise "like a pistol shot" when the fire ignited. By the time the Pascagoula Fire Department arrived, the plant was virtually destroyed. All twenty-five employees were able to escape without injury. One side of an old oak tree at the site still shows scars from this blaze. According to Jim Pelham, a local hunter who grew up near the decoy plant, the fire department dropped their hoses into the river to use the river water to extinguish the fire. However, there was so much sawdust from decoy production that it clogged the hoses. The fire smoldered for days until it burned completely out. The loss of the buildings, decoys, and equipment was estimated at $50,000. The machinery in the plant, which included a number of pattern-lathes, mill saws, power band saws, and other equipment, was only partially covered by insurance. Approximately 12,000 decoys valued at thousands of dollars continued to burn long after the main building collapsed into total ruin.

The lease on the buildings had been recently renewed with the Animal Trap Company and plans had been made to relocate the business to a larger facility in June 1947. This was necessary to accommodate the demand for decoys. However, as a result of the fire, the move was made earlier, in 1946, to a new facility located at the old airport hangar on Telephone Road in Pascagoula. During this time, Poitevin decided to retire, so management at corporate headquarters named Charles Weaver the new general manager. Weaver had been employed with the parent company in Pennsylvania for years and brought great experience with him to his new location in Pascagoula.

Animal Trap Company of Mississippi produced decoys of the following species: mallard, black duck, pintail, widgeon, blue-winged teal, canvasback, redhead, bluebill, goldeneye, goose, and mud hen. The decoys were

VICTOR DUCK DECOYS

FACTORY LIST PRICE

(All prices F.O.B. Factory)

FEBRUARY 1, 1946

Brand	Approx. Shipping Wt. Per Doz.	Price Per Dozen	F.O.B. Shipping Point
VICTOR VERI-LITE	18 lbs.	$14.40	Lititz, Pa.
VICTOR WOOD (Solid)	30 lbs.	14.40	Pascagoula, Miss.
VICTOR VAC STA	24 lbs.	16.00	Pascagoula, Miss.
VICTOR BALSA	18 lbs.	28.80	Pascagoula, Miss.

Packed—4 Drakes and 2 Hens per carton

VICTOR BALSA GOOSE DECOYS—Custom made on special order

Decoy Accessories

#1 VICTOR DECOY ANCHOR	12 lbs.	5.60	Lititz, Pa.
#1 VICTOR BALANCE WEIGHT	9 lbs.	3.40	Lititz, Pa.
#4 VICTOR MUSHROOM ANCHOR	7 lbs.	3.70	Lititz, Pa.
#4 VICTOR BODY BALANCE WEIGHT	4 lbs.	1.80	Lititz, Pa.

Send all orders to Lititz, Pa.

ANIMAL TRAP COMPANY of MISSISSIPPI

Subsidiary of

ANIMAL TRAP COMPANY of AMERICA

LITITZ, PENNSYLVANIA

PRINTED IN U.S.A.

1946 decoy price list.

The second location of the Animal Trap Company—the old airport hangar on Telephone Road. The company moved here after the fire of 1946 destroyed their Lake Avenue location. The factory stayed in operation until 1971. The building was torn down in September 2001.

primarily made from tupelo gum and pop ash wood; some were made of balsa in the 1950s. Earlier decoys were solid and hand-painted while later models were spray-painted; both had glass eyes that were first drilled then glued in place. Papier-mâché crow and owl decoys were made in the late 1940s and 1950s.

A distinguishing characteristic of Victor decoys is the lathe marks left by the duplicating machine. Most of the Number 12, economy grades had the name VICTOR branded on the bottom. The other wooden models had the name ANIMAL TRAP CO of MISS., INC. PASCAGOULA, MISS stamped on the bottom. The earlier decoys had a straight-line stamp while the later ones had a round one. Examples of each are pictured in this chapter.

Decoy accessories were also produced. Anchors and balance weights were available in cast iron and galvanized steel. The standard weight was seven to eight ounces and cost around $1 per dozen. Anchors were available in a loop and mushroom types. Balance weights had two nail holes for fastening to the bottom of the decoy. This balanced the bird so it would ride upright on the water. A four-ounce balance weight was added to the solid decoys, while a twelve-ounce was made for all the larger decoys. The VAC-STA decoys required no balance weights. Decoy anchor cord was supplied with all orders of decoy anchors and weights and was available in eight-foot sections.

A pair of No. 12 Victor mallards. Note the similarity to Poitevin's ideal grade (see chapter 5).

A No. 12 economy-grade black duck, Animal Trap Company. A thinner piece of wood was used for this model, which helped reduce the cost, originally about $5 a dozen.

An Animal Trap drake bluebill made in the 1950s.

In 1946, molded fiber or papier-mâché decoys were added to the product mix. Louie Gasaway, a former employee of the Animal Trap Company, described how the papier-mâché models were made:

> In the upstairs part of the building, bales of waxed, cardboard paper were mixed with water and rosin and fed into a pulp beader. Rosin held the pulp together. The product was tested for consistency and removed from the beader and transferred downstairs into tanks. The women employees took the product and placed it into a molder to shape into decoys. Afterwards, the ducks went into an oven to dry and then were painted.

These decoys were marketed under the brand name Victor Veri-Lite and had a paper label on the bottom identifying the bird as such. Some were branded with VICTOR VERI-LITE 1946 on the bottom. The papier-mâché decoys at one time had little value or interest to the decoy collector, but today, they are becoming very popular, as evidenced by the numbers bought and sold monthly on Ebay.

In the mid-1940s, the prairie pothole regions in Canada and key waterfowl-producing areas in the United States experienced drought conditions. The duck and goose populations started to decline to such levels that the federal authorities shortened the waterfowl seasons and reduced bag limits. Consequently, the demand for duck decoys dropped. In order to maintain full employment levels, Weaver announced in January 1948 that his company would start manufacturing roller skates. According to Weaver, production of wooden decoys in 1947 was below their record-breaking sales year of 1946. Another reason for the addition to their product line

Victor papier-mâché premier hen mallard, circa 1946.

Bottom view of a papier-mâché Victor Veri-Lite decoy with "Pascagoula" printed on the bottom.

was the decrease in sales of their animal traps. Weaver explained the decrease was the result of hurricane damage to key muskrat-producing marshes, which in turn adversely affected the number of trappers.

In 1952, the Animal Trap Company offered tenite decoys, which were made of hard plastic. The different models included Victor D-9 Standard Size, Victor D-10 Majestic, and Victor D-11 Majestic Oversize. During this same period, the Victor D-45 standard decoy was offered, which featured a wooden body with a removable tenite head. In 1958, the D-4 Imperial duck decoy was introduced and was the company's last effort to sell wooden decoys. This style featured an oversized, smooth-finished, all-wood decoy that was available in mallard, black duck, bluebill, widgeon, canvasback, and redhead species. By 1960, only mallards, canvasbacks, redheads, and bluebills were offered. The D-45 and D-4 Imperial models stayed on the market only until 1962. Hunters were more interested in the new, lightweight plastic decoys.

A Victor D-9 tenite mallard circa 1960s. This model replaced Animal Trap's popular papier-mâché decoys.

The Pascagoula plant continued wooden decoy production until 1962 and was one of the last companies in the United States to manufacture the wood versions. According to Weaver, the wood decoys made from the swamp hardwoods surprisingly had become collector's items. They were sold in gift shops for as high as $30 a duck, whereas the heyday wholesale price was $7.50 per dozen.

In 1966, the Animal Trap Company of America changed its name to Woodstream Corporation because of the variety of products turned out at the Lititz and Pascagoula plants, and a company that was in operation in Pascagoula for more than twenty-five years became only a memory. The new Woodstream plant sold plastic hunting and fishing supplies such as plastic decoys, Victor-20 slingshots, Old Pal minnow buckets, rods and reels, bait boxes, tackle boxes, and minnow traps.

In 1971, the Pascagoula plant was closed forever. The Woodstream Corporation, which is still in existence today in Lititz, Pennsylvania, consolidated plants around the country and moved their Mississippi operation to their plant in New Orleans.

A Victor D-9 plastic hen mallard circa 1966, Woodstream Corporation.

An original Animal Trap bluebill decoy made in the sleeping or preening position.

An Animal Trap drake mallard manufactured in the sleeping position.

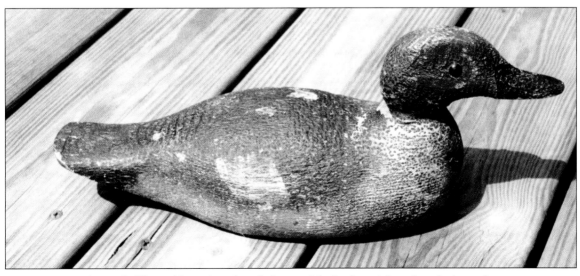

An early Victor blue-winged teal decoy with the breast bored and plugged, produced at the Lititz plant. This style decoy was made by the Pratt Manufacturing Company and briefly produced by the Animal Trap Company after the Pratt purchase in 1939.

A pair of No. 1 Animal Trap drake pintails circa 1940s.

A rare Animal Trap blue-winged teal drake in mint condition.

A bluebill decoy with the breast bored and plugged.

Bottom view displaying both the round and straight-line ANIMAL TRAP CO of MISS., INC. PASCAGOULA, MISS stamp.

An original pair of Animal Trap canvasbacks circa 1940s.

A rare American goldeneye decoy by the Animal Trap Company of Mississippi.

A VAC-STA black duck in original condition.

A pair of drake goldeneyes or whistlers, Animal Trap Company of Mississippi.

A decoy with the round stamp and the company's original No. 4 balance weight.

Victor coot or mud hen decoy circa 1950s.

Bottom view of the coot decoy showing the VICTOR name imprinted on the bottom

A pair of VAC-STA pintails in mint condition, Animal Trap Company.

A solid Animal Trap drake bluebill in original condition.

Drake redhead decoy, Animal Trap Company of Mississippi.

A Victor Junior duck decoy by the Animal Trap Company. These miniatures were eight inches in length and sold for $3 per dozen in 1939. Note the identical appearance to their regular-size mallard.

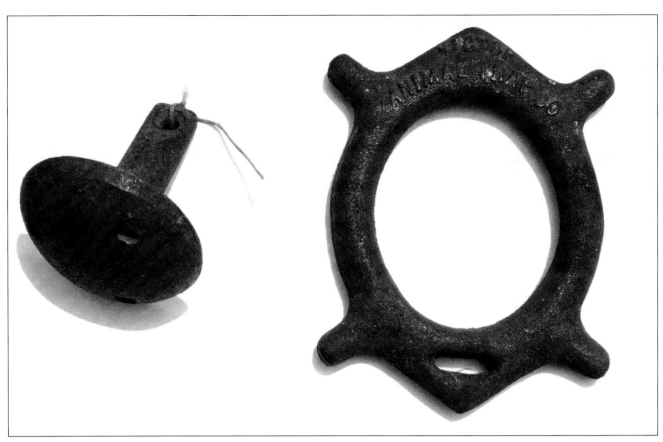

Victor No. 3 mushroom and No. 1 anchors circa 1940.

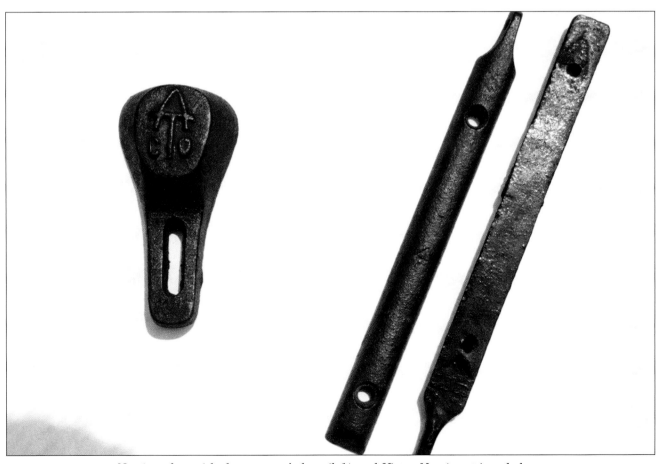

No. 1 anchor with the company's logo (left) and Victor No. 4 cast-iron balance weights.

An all-wood Victor D-4 Imperial hen mallard (top) and a D-2 papier-mâché mallard (bottom). The Imperial decoy was made in the late 1950s. It is obvious that the D-2 papier-mâché model was designed after the D-4 once the wooden version was discontinued.

Bottom of the D-4 Imperial decoy and head peg.

A Victor D-4 Imperial wooden drake canvasback circa 1950s.

Papier-mâché crow and owl set with the original box in mint condition, circa 1950s.

A Victor D-45 canvasback decoy with tenite head and wooden body circa 1952.

A Victor D-45 hen pintail circa 1952.

A Victor D-45 drake bluebill.

A rare Victor papier-mâché drake widgeon.

Papier-mâché premier mallard circa 1946, Animal Trap Company.

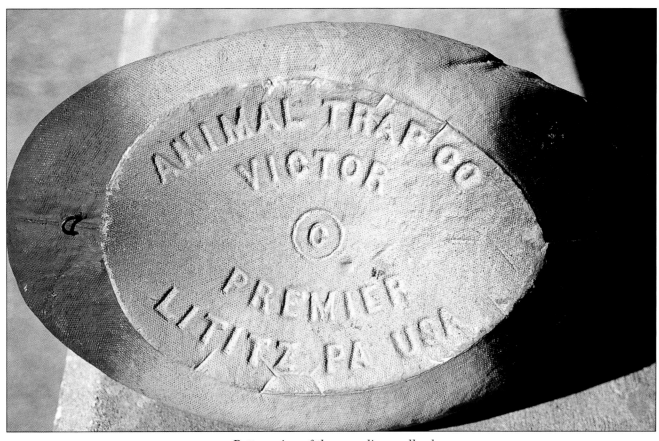

Bottom view of the preceding mallard.

A pair of Victor Veri-Lite, papier-mâché canvasbacks in original condition. These birds were made after the war in 1946.

Bottom view of a Victor Veri-Lite decoy branded and dated 1946, indicating when this style was first made. Some of these decoys had a paper war label on the bottom.

United States

NET WHOLESALE PRICES

—ON—

DECOY ACCESSORIES

June 1, 1939

(Subject to change without notice)

DECOY HEADS

Heads made from fine grained pine. This type of wood was selected after careful investigation and experiment. Heads with eyes, complete with dowel for replacing damaged heads, are available in all sizes and type. Packed — according to orders. Sizes either Nos. 1, 2 or 12. Be sure to specify type of duck and finish for which heads are being ordered. Also specify whether heads are for drake or hen.

Price per dozen $2.50

EYES

DECOY EYES

Supplied for all types. Specify type of decoy for which eyes are desired.

Price per dozen pairs . . . . $ .30

DECOY ANCHORS

No. 1A — Cast Iron — So designed that after cord has been wound around neck, large anchor loop can be slipped over head of decoy for storing. Weight each 7 ounces.

Price per dozen . . . . $ .70

No. 1B — Galvanized — Same style as No. 1A except for finish.

Price per dozen . . . . $ .90

No. 1A and No. 1B

No. 4A — Mushroom type — Cast Iron with hole in upright stem for tying cord. Weight each 8 ounces.

Price per dozen . . . . $ .90

No. 4B — Same mushroom type as No. 4A except for size. Weight each 18 ounces.

Price per dozen $2.00

No. 4A and No. 4B

BALANCE WEIGHTS FOR DECOYS

Cast Iron with eyelets for anchor cord. Two nail holes for fastening weight to decoy. These weights are easily attached and will balance the decoy so it will set upright properly in water. Cheaper than lead strips and no trouble to attach.

No. 4 — Japanned finish — For all standard solid decoys. Packed 1 dozen to a box, weight each 4 ounces.

Price per dozen . . . . $ .75

No. 5 — Japanned finish — For all hollow and larger decoys. Packed 1 dozen to a box, weight each 12 ounces.

Price per dozen $1.25

No. 4 and No. 5

No. 6 — Cast Iron — Fitted with lugs so weight may be fastened to decoys. Made like keel of a boat. Will keep decoy upright in rough water. Packed 1 dozen to a box, weight each 4 ounces.

Price per dozen . . . . $ .65

No. 6

DECOY ANCHOR CORD

Supplied with all orders for decoy anchors and weights. Twelve only, 8 foot cords in each package.

Dealers and sportsmen should be notified by wholesalers' salesmen that we maintain a service for repairing, repainting and replacing of broken heads, damaged or missing eyes. Write for quotations, giving details of necessary repairs. Quotations will be mailed same day request is received. All work properly handled.

ANIMAL TRAP COMPANY OF AMERICA

LITITZ, PA.

See other side for Price List and Description of Decoys

Victor

DECOYS AND ACCESSORIES

For the Hunter Who Demands the Finest

Victor offers you true, life-like decoys. Broad-body realism; painted in natural colors; waterproof. Molded fiber and plastic duck decoys are internally balanced and self-righting. Equipped with anchor line attachment plus other wanted features that make Victor the finest decoy line.

No. D-3 Victor Magnum. Light, tough molded fiber. Glass eyes. • Mallard, Black Duck, Red Head, Blue Bill, Canvasback, Whistler, Widgeon, Pintail, Teal.
Packed: 8—16 lbs.; 6—11 lbs.
$9.85 Per Doz.
$8.80 Per 8 Pak

Victor MOLDED FIBER

No. D-2 Victor Premier. Slightly smaller than the Magnum. • Mallard, Black Duck, Pintail, Red Head, Canvasback, Blue Bill. Packed: 8—14 lbs.; 6—9 lbs.
$8.85 Per Doz.
$6.80 Per 8 Pak

No. D-0 Victor Veri-Lite. Low-priced for occasional hunters. Life-size. Glass eyes. • Mallard, Black Duck, Pintail.
Packed: ½ doz.—10 lbs.
$7.75 Per Doz.

Victor PLASTIC

No. D-9 Victor Majestic Champion. One-piece, life-size, Tenite plastic decoy. Molded keel adds stability for natural action. • Mallard, Pintail, Black Duck, Blue Bill, Canvasback.
Packed: ½ doz.—6½ lbs.
$10.85 Per Doz.

No. D-10 Victor Majestic Standard. Life-size, Tenite plastic. Molded eyes. Detachable and adjustable all-position head. • Mallard, Black Duck, Pintail, Canvasback, Blue Bill, Red Head, Ring-necked (Ring-bill), Whistler.
Packed: ½ doz.—8 lbs.
$14.85 Per Doz.

No. D-11 Victor Majestic Oversize. Deluxe, Tenite plastic. Detachable head. Ideal for open water shooting. • Mallard, Black Duck, Pintail, Canvasback, Blue Bill, Red Head.
Packed: ½ doz.—15 lbs.
$23.00 Per Doz.

Victor POLYETHYLENE PLASTIC

No. D-95. Self-inflating—works like a plastic squeeze bottle. Not affected by extreme temperatures. Shot resistant. • Mallard, Black Duck, Pintail. Packed: ½ doz.—4 lbs.
$12.00 Per Doz.

All duck decoys packed half drakes, half hens to a carton.

May 1962 Victor decoys and accessories price list. The company stopped wooden decoy production in 1962.

No. D-4 Victor Imperial. Oversize. Finest wood decoy on the market. Glass eyes. Authentic colors. Mallard, Black Duck, Pintail. ~~DISCONTINUED~~ **$25.00 Per Doz.** Packed: ½ doz.—18½ lbs.

Victor WOOD

No. D-45 Victor Standard. Detachable, Tenite plastic head. • Mallard, Black Duck, Canvasback, Pintail, Redhead, Bluebill. ~~DISCONTINUED~~ **$16.50 Per Doz.** Packed: ½ doz.—17 lbs.

Victor FIELD DECOY

No. D-1. Molded fiber. Sturdy, full-size decoy for field shooting. • Mallard, Black Duck, Pintail.
Packed: 1 doz.—8 lbs. **$6.95 Per Doz.**

Victor DELUXE CANADA GOOSE

No. D-12. Full-size, three-dimensional. Pressed fiber, realistically painted. Converts to floating decoy for water use. Floating, feeding and upright heads supplied.
Packed: ½ doz.—9 lbs. **$19.95 Per Doz.**

D-1, D-5 and D-12 bodies nest together for convenient carrying and minimum storage. Heads and stakes fit inside body.

Victor CANADA GOOSE

No. D-5. Molded fiber decoy for field use. Adjustable upright and feeder heads. Converts for water use with stake extension. • Canada, Snow and Blue Goose.
Packed: ½ doz.—7½ lbs. **$13.95 Per Doz.**

Victor OWL

No. D-7. Great horned owl. Life-size, molded fiber reproduction for attracting crows. Large, fierce-looking glass eyes.
Packed: ⅓ doz.—6 lbs.

$17.25 Per Doz.

Victor CROW and OWL SET

No. D-8. Perfect gift for crow shooters.
Packed: 2 Crows, 1 Owl—5½ lbs.

$34.00 Per Doz.

Victor CROW

No. D-6. Molded fiber. Attracts crows into easy shotgun range. Wire legs. Convenient opening for attaching to tree limb.
Packed: ½ doz.—4½ lbs. **$8.75 Per Doz.**

RECORDED FOWL and ANIMAL CALLS

The original 45 RPM records for game callers. Actual recordings of live birds and animals. Eight records: D-100 Black and Mallard Ducks; D-101 Pintails, Mixed Black and Mallard Ducks; C-100 Crows (feeding and riot call); C-101 Crows (young and nesting); C-102 Crows (fighting and distress calls); G-200 Geese; T-300 Wild Turkeys; P-400 Rabbit Squeal (for foxes, wolves, owls, wildcats). **$15.00 Per Doz.**

Note: Current regulations in U.S. and Canada prohibit use of recorded calls for shooting migratory waterfowl.

Victor ACCESSORIES

	Packed	Weight	Per Doz.
No. 1 Victor Decoy Anchor, 1 lb.	1 doz.	13 lbs.	$3.25
No. 2 Victor Decoy Anchor, 2 lb.	1 doz.	25 lbs.	5.50
No. 3 Victor Mushroom Anchor, 8 oz.	1 doz.	7 lbs.	2.75
No. 4 Victor Balance Weight, 8 oz.	1 doz.	7 lbs.	2.25
No. 5 Victor Balance Weight, 4 oz.	1 doz.	4 lbs.	1.80

No. 1
No. 2
No. 4
No. 3
No. 5

Old Pal FOLDING SEAT

No. 40. Compact; holds up to 240 lbs. Plated steel frame; heavy Army duck seat.
Packed: 1 doz.—23 lbs.

$12.96 Per Doz.

ANIMAL TRAP COMPANY OF AMERICA \ Lititz, Pa. • Pascagoula, Miss. Niagara Falls, Canada

Printed in U.S.A.

INO—15M—5/15/62

Victor

DECOYS AND ACCESSORIES

For the Shooter Who Demands the Finest in Fiber Decoys

D-3 MALLARD HEN

D-3 MALLARD DRAKE

Victor MOLDED FIBER

No. D-3 Victor Magnum

Now Victor offers you the true, real-life decoy. The new Victor Magnum sits lower in the water, is broader across the back, gives a more lifelike appearance to highflying game. Built of light, tough molded fiber, painted in natural lifelike colors. Glass eyes. Mallard has head and wings painted with iridescent paint for added realism and attraction. Victor Molded Fiber Decoys are thoroughly waterproof and self-righting. Equipped with anchor line staple . . . simply tie on line and they're ready to use. Nine species: Mallard, Black Duck, Red Head, Blue Bill, Canvasback, Whistler, Widgeon, Pintail, Teal.

Packed and weight per carton: 8 — 16 lbs.; 6 — 11 lbs.

No. D-2 Victor Premier

Offers the same new, broad-body realism and features of the Victor Magnum but slightly smaller. Pre-balanced and waterproof. Mallard has head and wings painted with iridescent paint. Six species: Mallard, Black Duck, Pintail, Red Head, Canvasback, Blue Bill.

Packed and weight per carton: 8 — 14 lbs.; 6 — 9 lbs.

BLACK DUCK   **RED HEAD**   **BLUE BILL**

CANVASBACK   **WHISTLER**   **WIDGEON**

PINTAIL   **TEAL**

D-2 MALLARD

BLACK DUCK   **CANVASBACK**   **RED HEAD**

PINTAIL   **BLUE BILL**

Victor Decoys and Accessories catalog, circa 1950s.

Victor PLASTIC

No. D-10 Victor Majestic Standard

Life-size, Tenite plastic decoy, internally balanced. Waterproof, and finished in realistic colors. Adjustable, all-position head with molded eyes. Mallard has head and wings painted with iridescent paint. Four places for anchor line attachment. Seven species: Mallard, Black Duck, Pintail, Canvasback, Blue Bill, Red Head, Ring-necked (Ring-bill).

Packed and weight per carton: 6—8 lbs.

Adjustable, all-position head on Standard and Oversize styles can be permanently attached according to the shooter's preference. Adhesive supplied in each carton.

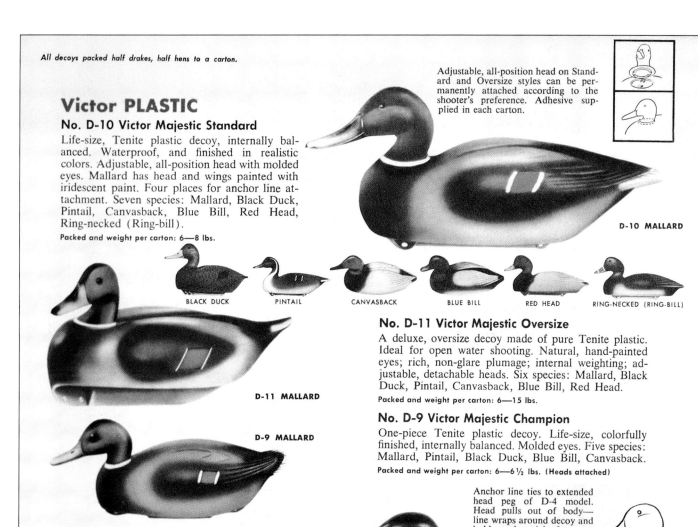

D-10 MALLARD

BLACK DUCK   PINTAIL   CANVASBACK   BLUE BILL   RED HEAD   RING-NECKED (RING-BILL)

D-11 MALLARD

D-9 MALLARD

No. D-11 Victor Majestic Oversize

A deluxe, oversize decoy made of pure Tenite plastic. Ideal for open water shooting. Natural, hand-painted eyes; rich, non-glare plumage; internal weighting; adjustable, detachable heads. Six species: Mallard, Black Duck, Pintail, Canvasback, Blue Bill, Red Head.

Packed and weight per carton: 6—15 lbs.

No. D-9 Victor Majestic Champion

One-piece Tenite plastic decoy. Life-size, colorfully finished, internally balanced. Molded eyes. Five species: Mallard, Pintail, Black Duck, Blue Bill, Canvasback.

Packed and weight per carton: 6—6½ lbs. (Heads attached)

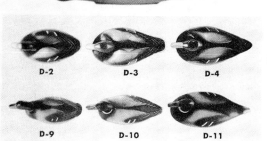

D-2   D-3   D-4

D-9   D-10   D-11

"Duck's-Eye View." Note the broad backs, the over-all length and the natural, sculptured plumage of these new Victor decoys.

Anchor line ties to extended head peg of D-4 model. Head pulls out of body—line wraps around decoy and holds anchor tight for compact storage. This also eliminates the cause of much bill and neck breakage.

D-4 MALLARD

Victor MOLDED FIBER

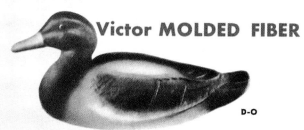

D-O

No. D-O Veri-Lite

A low-price decoy especially designed for "occasional" hunters whose requirements are less exacting. Full life-size. Pre-balanced and waterproofed. Tough molded fiber body fully hardened and colorfully painted. Glass eyes; anchor line staple. Three species: Mallard, Black Duck, Pintail.

Packed and weight per carton: 6—10 lbs.

Victor WOOD No. D-4 Victor Imperial

Here, without doubt, is the finest wood decoy on the market today. It offers the new Victor broad-back look. In addition, the Victor Imperial creates an amazing, true-to-life head movement on the water. The oversize body is made of selected wood finished in authentic colors. Mallard has head and wings painted with iridescent paint. Glass eyes. Six species: Mallard, Black Duck, Canvasback, Red Head, Blue Bill, Widgeon.

Packed and weight per carton: 6—18½ lbs.

No. D-45 Victor Standard

D-45 MALLARD

Sturdy, life-size model painted in authentic, non-glare colors to give a realistic "feather" effect. Detachable Tenite plastic head. Nine species: Mallard, Black Duck, Canvasback, Pintail, Teal, Red Head, Whistler, Blue Bill, Widgeon.

Packed and weight per carton: 6—17 lbs.

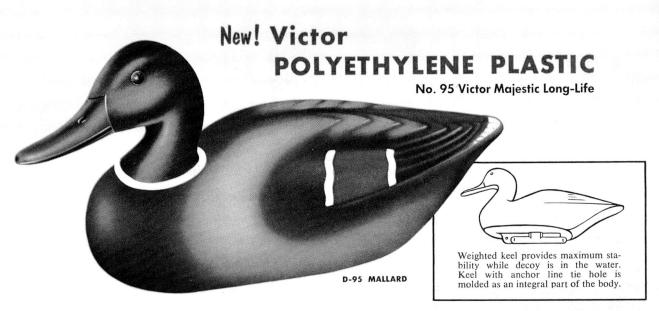

New! Victor
POLYETHYLENE PLASTIC

No. 95 Victor Majestic Long-Life

D-95 MALLARD

Weighted keel provides maximum stability while decoy is in the water. Keel with anchor line tie hole is molded as an integral part of the body.

This new Victor Majestic Long-Life decoy is a natural for duck hunters who demand top quality, maximum convenience and sure results. Molded of pliable polyethylene plastic, it is self-inflating, has no complicated valves—works like a plastic squeeze bottle. This brand new decoy is designed to last a lifetime. It is not affected by extremes of hot or cold temperature; is life-size and has realistic molded eyes. It is unusually light in weight, pre-balanced and equipped with anchor line tie. The No. 95 rides free and lifelike on the water, is waterproof and shot resistant. Painted in natural non-glare colors. Three species: Mallard, Black Duck and Pintail.

Packed and weight per carton: 6 — 8 lbs.

New! Portable Hi-Fi Bird And Animal Caller
"Call of the Wild"

Now you can use actual recorded calls to attract ducks, geese, crows, wild turkey, fox, coyote, wildcat and other predators into close shooting range. (Note: Current regulations in United States and Canada prohibit use for shooting migratory waterfowl.)

Call of the Wild is a portable, three-speed record player with a powerful transistor amplifier that can be heard up to a distance of three miles. Transistors and printed circuits eliminate the use of vibrators and other fragile and expensive parts. Rugged construction assures long, trouble-free performance.

Sportsmen's and conservation clubs, game commissions and wildlife agencies use Call of the Wild for predator control and to call ducks, geese and turkeys for banding.

The unit is compact, light in weight, and fully weather-proof. It is powered by inexpensive dry cell batteries which last for many hours of operation. Over-all size—9" x 11" x 6¼"; shipping weight (less batteries)—17 lbs.

Seven 45 RPM records are available: D-100 Ducks (black ducks and mallards on both sides); D-101 Ducks (pintails on one side, mixed black ducks and mallards on reverse side); C-100 Crows (feeding and riot call); C-101 Crows (young and nesting); G-200 Geese; T-300 Wild Turkeys; P-400 Squealing Rabbit (for foxes, wolves, owls, wildcats).

"Call of the Wild" is ideal for use as a low-cost public address system by simply plugging in hand microphone (optional at low extra cost).

SOCIAL FUNCTIONS

ATHLETIC EVENTS

SPORTS CLUBS

YACHT CLUBS

HUNTING CAMPS

EMERGENCY CALLING

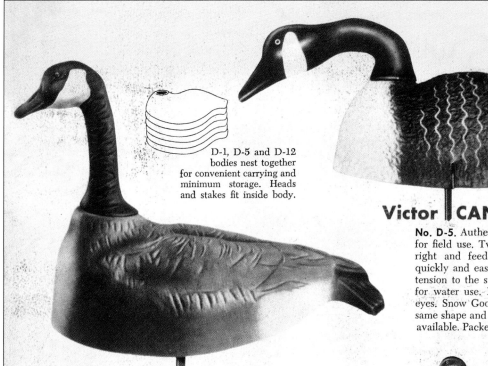

D-1, D-5 and D-12 bodies nest together for convenient carrying and minimum storage. Heads and stakes fit inside body.

Victor CANADA GOOSE

No. D-5. Authentic, molded fiber decoy designed for field use. Two types of adjustable heads, upright and feeder. Heads can be interchanged quickly and easily in the field. By adding an extension to the stake, the decoy can be converted for water use. Feather finish with genuine glass eyes. Snow Goose and Blue Goose decoys in the same shape and size as the Canada Goose are also available. Packed ½ doz.; wt. 7½ lbs.

Victor FIELD DECOY

No. D-1. A sturdy, full-size duck decoy especially designed for field shooting. Construction similar to D-5 goose. Three species: Mallard, Black Duck, Pintail. Packed and weight per carton: 12—8 lbs.

Victor DELUXE CANADA GOOSE

No. D-12. Full-size, three-dimensional decoy of rigid, pressed fiber construction, realistically painted. Spring clip holds head securely to body. Field decoy converts to floating decoy by adding a wood board. Feeding and upright heads supplied. Packed ½ doz.; wt. 9 lbs.

Victor CROW

No. D-6. Victor Crow decoy will attract curious crows into easy shotgun range. Wire legs for setting in field. Also has convenient opening for attaching to tree limb. Packed ½ doz.; wt. 4½ lbs.

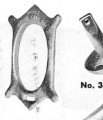

Victor OWL

No. D-7. Actual reproduction of a great horned owl. Large fierce-looking glass eyes. Crows cannot resist attacking this villain. Packed ⅓ doz.; wt. 6 lbs.

Victor CROW and OWL SET

No. D-8. A popular crow shooter's kit consisting of two crows and one owl. A perfect gift for hunters. Wt. 5½ lbs.

Victor CRO-TONE CALL

No. D-13. Crow call made of oil-impregnated birch and fitted with Pennsylvania cedar reed holders. Authentic tone; convenient lanyard supplied. Packed 1 doz. per counter display; wt. 1 lb.

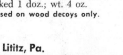

No. 1
No. 2
No. 3
No. 4
No. 5

Victor ACCESSORIES

No. 1 and No. 2 Victor Anchors. Unreel lines automatically as tide rises. Packed 1 doz.; wts. No. 1, 14 oz.; No. 2, 2 lbs.
No. 3 Victor Mushroom Anchor. Popular, dependable. Packed 1 doz.; wt. 8 oz.
No. 4 Victor Balance Weight. One screw fastens weight to body. Prongs prevent balance from changing position. Packed 1 doz.; wt. 8 oz.
No. 5 Victor Balance Weight. Attaches to decoy with two nails or screws. Eyelet for anchor line. Packed 1 doz.; wt. 4 oz.
Balance weights used on wood decoys only.

ANIMAL TRAP COMPANY OF AMERICA

Lititz, Pa.
Pascagoula, Miss.
Niagara Falls, Canada

RG-10M-759

For a close-up Shot... Set Out Victor Decoys

THERE'S A VICTOR DECOY FOR EVERY SHOOTER'S NEEDS!

VICTOR MAJESTIC CHAMPION

A new, popular-priced, one-piece Tenite plastic decoy, authentically reproducing Mallard, Pintail or Black Duck species. The Champion is life-size, internally balanced and colorfully finished. (Victor Majestic Standard and Oversize Models also available.)

VICTOR TRU-LIFE

Realistic, life-size decoy of light, tough, molded fiber. Prebalanced and waterproof. Permanent head. Mallard and Black Duck species available. (Victor Veri-Lite series also available in 9 species.)

VICTOR DELUXE CANADA GOOSE

Full-sized, three-dimensional goose decoy for field use; converts to a floating decoy by adding a wood board. Rigid fiber, realistically molded and painted. Feeding and upright heads supplied. (Standard model also available.)

SEE YOUR VICTOR DEALER

for his complete line of Victor Calls, Owl and Crow Decoys, and other accessories.

ANIMAL TRAP COMPANY OF AMERICA, Dept. 304
Lititz, Pa. • Pascagoula, Miss. • Niagara Falls, Canada

Ad from Field & Stream, *November 1955.*

Victor Decoys

"Thoroughbreds", that's what they are!

Whatever the sport, every true sportsman appreciates the "thoroughbred"—the finest! For realism, for effectiveness, Victor decoys rate tops with hunters who insist on the best.

New! Victor Molded Fiber

No. D-3 Victor Magnum Designed to sit lower in the water, broader across the back, gives a more life-like appearance to high-flying game. Natural, life-like colors. Oversize for greater attraction.

No. D-2 Victor Premier Same realistic appearance as No. D-3; slightly smaller.

Victor Majestic Plastic

No. D-10 Standard Life-size, Tenite plastic. Adjustable, all-position head; waterproof; finished in realistic colors.

No. D-9 Victor Majestic Champion One-piece Tenite plastic. Life-size.

No. D-11 Victor Majestic Oversize A deluxe, oversize decoy made of pure Tenite plastic. Ideal for open water shooting.

New! Victor Wood

No. D-4 Victor Imperial For those who prefer the qualities of wood. Has the new Victor broad-back look plus actual, true-to-life head and body movement on the water.

ANIMAL TRAP COMPANY OF AMERICA
Lititz, Pa. • Pascagoula, Miss. • Niagara Falls, Canada

Ad from Field & Stream, *August 1957.*

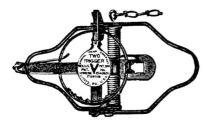
Ad from Hunting & Fishing Magazine, October 1944.

Ad from Hardware World, March 1952.

WOODSTREAM
CORPORATION

LITITZ, PENNSYLVANIA 17543
TELEPHONE AREA CODE 717 / 626-2125

 ANIMAL TRAP COMPANY
OF AMERICA

 OLD PAL INC.

 WORTH FIBRE CO.

TRAPPE INC.

J. I. ANTHONY
VICE PRESIDENT
MANUFACTURING

June 14, 1966

Mr. C. W. Ford
Ford, Moore & Jones
P. O. Box 100
Pascagoula, Mississippi 39576

Dear Mr. Ford:

Enclosed is another claim from Sears Roebuck store. I'm
also sending you a copy of the machinery and equipment
values which we completely overlooked in the preparation
of our suit against Chemfax.

You'll notice that our depreciated value totals $6614.21
and certainly should be added to our damages, since this
equipment is worthless to us now.

Sincerely yours,

WOODSTREAM CORPORATION

J. I. Anthony
Vice Pres., Mfg.

JIA:mcw

Enclosures

*Woodstream Corporation letterhead. This letter involved a lawsuit filed by the
Animal Trap Company against Chemfax of Gulfport, Mississippi. Animal Trap
claimed the chemical impregnator used for waterproofing the papier-mâché
decoys produced a nauseating odor that resulted in loss of business. In 1966, the
Animal Trap Company changed their name to Woodstream Corporation.*

HOW TO USE
DUCK DECOYS
Successfully

ANIMAL TRAP COMPANY OF MISSISSIPPI

Subsidiary of

ANIMAL TRAP COMPANY OF AMERICA

Lititz, Penna.　　—　　Niagara Falls, Ont.

Front of company brochure, circa 1945.

VAC STA DECOYS

(Patent No. 1,708,762)

VAC STA MALLARD　　　SEE THE VACUUM CUPS

Vac Sta decoys are made as illustrated above with twin air spaces which balance the decoy without necessity of weights.

Vac Sta decoys look alive—they almost swim in a breeze or tide.

Vac Sta decoys are high grade Hudson pattern, machine made decoys and are turned out of selected water resisting wood from the Singing River County of Mississippi.

Vac Sta decoys will bring ducks into the blind. They are painted in natural colors and designed right. Furnished in feather finish—no glare, in the following species: Mallard—Red Head—Canvasback—Pintail—Blue Bill—Black Duck—Teal—Widgeon—Whistler—Mud Hen.

Packed 4 Drakes, 2 Hens per case

Shipping Weight 8¼ pounds per ½ dozen

Shipped from Pascagoula, Mississippi

DUCK HUNTERS——HELP YOUR SPORT

No organization of sportsmen is doing more for the restoration of our waterfowl and the sport of wildfowling than Ducks Unlimited, Inc. Every real duck hunter can help this national wildfowler's organization by becoming a member. Write Ducks Unlimited, Inc., 342 Madison Avenue, New York 17, N. Y. for membership literature.

Back of company brochure, circa 1945.

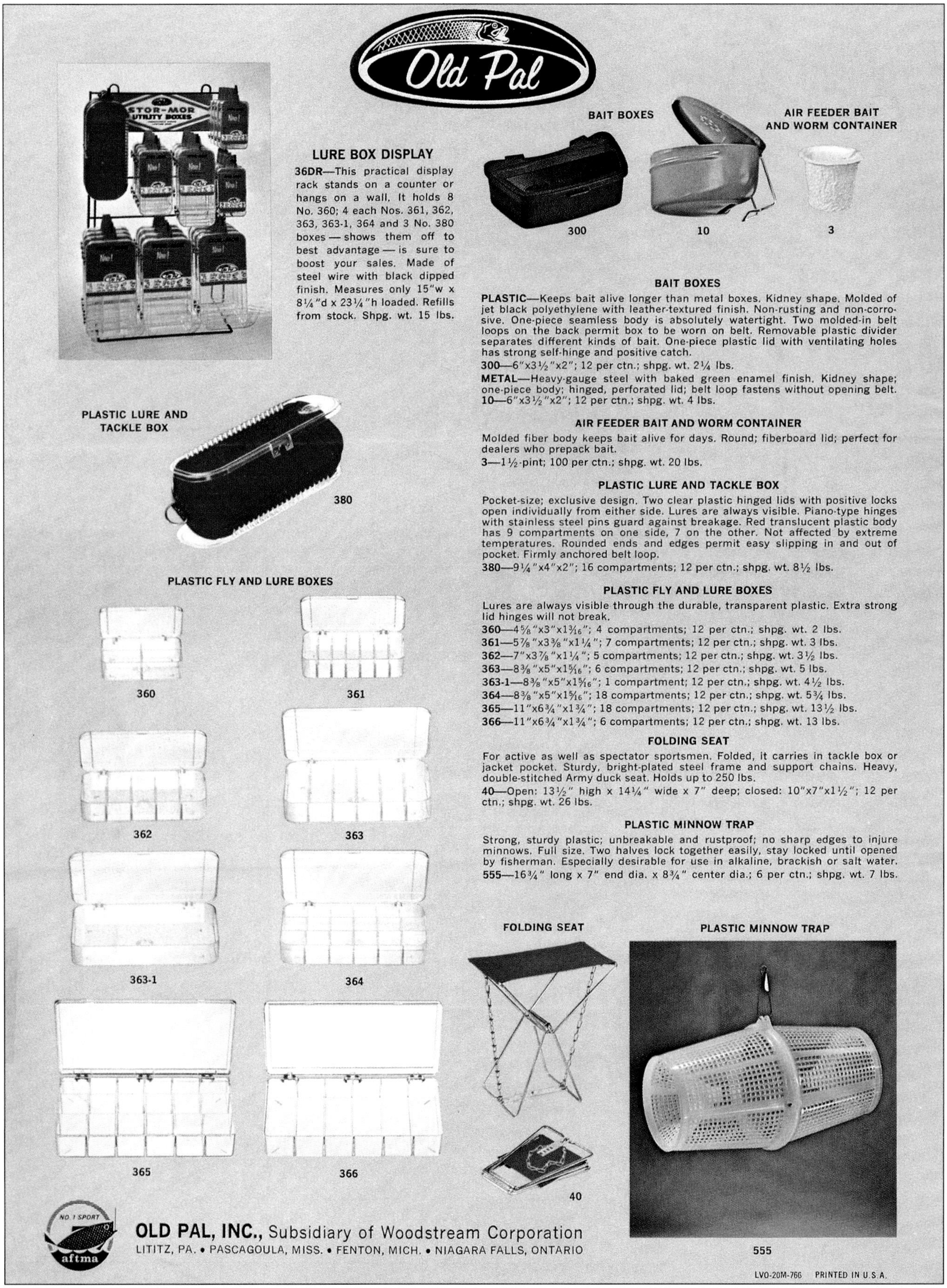

BAIT BOXES

AIR FEEDER BAIT AND WORM CONTAINER

300

10

3

LURE BOX DISPLAY

36DR—This practical display rack stands on a counter or hangs on a wall, It holds 8 No. 360; 4 each Nos. 361, 362, 363, 363-1, 364 and 3 No. 380 boxes — shows them off to best advantage — is sure to boost your sales. Made of steel wire with black dipped finish. Measures only 15"w x 8¼"d x 23¼"h loaded. Refills from stock. Shpg. wt. 15 lbs.

BAIT BOXES

PLASTIC—Keeps bait alive longer than metal boxes. Kidney shape. Molded of jet black polyethylene with leather-textured finish. Non-rusting and non-corrosive. One-piece seamless body is absolutely watertight. Two molded-in belt loops on the back permit box to be worn on belt. Removable plastic divider separates different kinds of bait. One-piece plastic lid with ventilating holes has strong self-hinge and positive catch.
300—6"x3½"x2"; 12 per ctn.; shpg. wt. 2¼ lbs.
METAL—Heavy-gauge steel with baked green enamel finish. Kidney shape; one-piece body; hinged, perforated lid; belt loop fastens without opening belt.
10—6"x3½"x2"; 12 per ctn.; shpg. wt. 4 lbs.

AIR FEEDER BAIT AND WORM CONTAINER

Molded fiber body keeps bait alive for days. Round; fiberboard lid; perfect for dealers who prepack bait.
3—1½-pint; 100 per ctn.; shpg. wt. 20 lbs.

PLASTIC LURE AND TACKLE BOX

Pocket-size; exclusive design. Two clear plastic hinged lids with positive locks open individually from either side. Lures are always visible. Piano-type hinges with stainless steel pins guard against breakage. Red translucent plastic body has 9 compartments on one side, 7 on the other. Not affected by extreme temperatures. Rounded ends and edges permit easy slipping in and out of pocket. Firmly anchored belt loop.
380—9¼"x4"x2"; 16 compartments; 12 per ctn.; shpg. wt. 8½ lbs.

PLASTIC LURE AND TACKLE BOX

380

PLASTIC FLY AND LURE BOXES

Lures are always visible through the durable, transparent plastic. Extra strong lid hinges will not break.
360—4⅝"x3"x1³⁄₁₆"; 4 compartments; 12 per ctn.; shpg. wt. 2 lbs.
361—5⅞"x3⅜"x1¼"; 7 compartments; 12 per ctn.; shpg. wt. 3 lbs.
362—7"x3⅞"x1¼"; 5 compartments; 12 per ctn.; shpg. wt. 3½ lbs.
363—8⅜"x5"x1⁵⁄₁₆"; 6 compartments; 12 per ctn.; shpg. wt. 5 lbs.
363-1—8⅜"x5"x1⁵⁄₁₆"; 1 compartment; 12 per ctn.; shpg. wt. 4½ lbs.
364—8⅜"x5"x1⁵⁄₁₆"; 18 compartments; 12 per ctn.; shpg. wt. 5¾ lbs.
365—11"x6¾"x1¾"; 18 compartments; 12 per ctn.; shpg. wt. 13½ lbs.
366—11"x6¾"x1¾"; 6 compartments; 12 per ctn.; shpg. wt. 13 lbs.

FOLDING SEAT

For active as well as spectator sportsmen. Folded, it carries in tackle box or jacket pocket. Sturdy, bright-plated steel frame and support chains. Heavy, double-stitched Army duck seat. Holds up to 250 lbs.
40—Open: 13½" high x 14¼" wide x 7" deep; closed: 10"x7"x1½"; 12 per ctn.; shpg. wt. 26 lbs.

PLASTIC MINNOW TRAP

Strong, sturdy plastic; unbreakable and rustproof; no sharp edges to injure minnows. Full size. Two halves lock together easily, stay locked until opened by fisherman. Especially desirable for use in alkaline, brackish or salt water.
555—16¾" long x 7" end dia. x 8¾" center dia.; 6 per ctn.; shpg. wt. 7 lbs.

PLASTIC FLY AND LURE BOXES

360

361

362

363

363-1

364

365

366

FOLDING SEAT

40

PLASTIC MINNOW TRAP

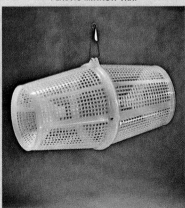

555

OLD PAL, INC., Subsidiary of Woodstream Corporation
LITITZ, PA. • PASCAGOULA, MISS. • FENTON, MICH. • NIAGARA FALLS, ONTARIO

LVO-20M-766   PRINTED IN U.S.A.

Back page of a 1967 Old Pal catalog, listing fishing supplies offered by the Woodstream Corporation.

CHAPTER 9

PASCAGOULA DECOY COMPANY

Lester Clarence Winterton was born on November 5, 1895. A self-educated man, he was a consulting engineer and was employed as a civil engineer with the city of Pascagoula. Winterton was considered a visionary and one of the most progressive-thinking engineers the city ever had. He married Josie Gautier of Pascagoula, and the couple resided in Gautier, Mississippi.

In June 1940, Winterton and Clifford L. Dees of Vancleave, Mississippi started the Pascagoula Decoy Company at 831 North Pascagoula Street (where the Pavco Veneer Mill is today). On April 15, 1941, the company started to grow by purchasing the machinery and rough-cut decoys from the Trehern Decoy Factory. In 1943, Winterton solely acquired the business from Dees and purchased the Avery Plywood Company and Martin Veneer Mill on North Pascagoula Street. With the additional space and buildings, the business was able to expand and prosper.

The Pascagoula Decoy Company produced quality wooden products that found wide patronage throughout the country. The company produced wooden waterfowl decoys and sold them under the brand name PADCO. They also manufactured miter boxes, saw handles, hardwood flooring, wooden shoes, varnished oars and paddles, skiffs, duck boats, boat hooks, and even oak mast hoops for sailboats. During their peak production era, they employed more than two hundred people.

The decoys were made from native pop ash and tupelo gum. The wood, mostly provided by Cumbest Manufacturing in precut, 4x8-inch blocks, was transported by rail and truck to the plant. The blocks were turned on the lathe machine and afterwards put in a motor-operated barrel that slowly rotated. This sanding effect reduced the amount of time employees spent hand-sanding the decoys. Up to 360 decoys were produced daily. The decoys had solid bodies, glass eyes, and flat bottoms and were hand-painted. These were distinguishable characteristics of PADCO birds. The decoys also had the rough finish with marks encircling the body and head left by the duplicating lathe machines. The design was simple, yet the decoys rode beautifully on the water and did not pop up and down in rough weather conditions as the plastic versions did.

Women employees of the Pascagoula Decoy Company painting the decoys on an assembly line.

Decoy bodies turned on the lathe machines and placed in storage. Next, the band saw trimmed the blocks and then they were ready for priming and painting.

The products made by the Pascagoula Decoy Company were the best money could buy, and this was recognized by sportsmen, and now collectors, across the country. Shipments were made all over the United States, Canada, Mexico, and Switzerland. They supplied their products on a wholesale level to jobbers and dealers, a retail level to sporting-goods stores, and to catalog companies such as Sears Roebuck & Company and Montgomery Ward. According to the late Dr. Perry Thompson, a local hunter who once used PADCO products throughout the 1940s and 1950s, "their decoys were quality-made, durable, and the resemblance to real ducks was second to none. I've used their products for decades and achieved great results."

The ten different species produced were mallard, black duck, baldpate, pintail, bluebill, goldeneye, canvasback, redhead, ring-neck, and coot or poule-d'eau. Miniature decoys were made in mallard, black duck, and pintail drakes and served as salesman samples, toys, paperweights, and promotional items such as ashtrays and desktop lamps. According to the late Charles Ford, an avid sportsman from Pascagoula, the Pascagoula

A pair of PADCO standard-grade mallards in original condition.

Decoy Company produced wooden goose decoys upon special request from clients. Decoys were made in supreme, top flight, standard, and special grades, and a detailed explanation of each is provided in the company's catalog.

The Pascagoula Decoy Company was a direct competitor of the Animal Trap Company. Both companies differentiated themselves with advertisements in national sporting magazines, such as *Outdoor Life* and *Field & Stream*. While the two factory styles closely resembled each other, a distinguishing characteristic between the two is the diameter of the dowel. A half-inch wooden dowel attached the heads of the PADCO decoys, and the Animal Trap used a five-eighths-inch. The paint styles and designs were also different, which is evident when you compare photographs of similar species produced by the two companies.

The Pascagoula Decoy Company played a significant role in the United States' efforts during World War II. In 1943, they entered into contracts with the government to produce wooden paddles and oars, ammunition boxes, and ladder rungs for the navy ships. These products and supplies were made for the United States Navy, Army, and Coast Guard. During this period, duck decoy production completely stopped, and the company had only a limited supply in stock. After the war, the company continued to manufacture their complete product line.

In October 1948, a fire of undetermined origin broke out in the decoy-producing section of the warehouse and destroyed the building filled with

Ad from Outdoor Life Magazine, *October 1942.*

Ad from Jackson County Business & Civic Guide, *1946.*

finished duck decoys. The piles of sawdust and the heart-pine internal construction of the sheet-metal-framed building rapidly went up in flames. The damage was estimated at $50,000. Fortunately, no one was injured in the fire, which was contained by the Pascagoula Fire Department before spreading to a nearby building that housed the expensive machinery. The other departments of the company absorbed the decoy-production employees until operation was restored. The Pascagoula Decoy Company literally had a "fire sale" to the public of the surviving but damaged birds. A dozen decoys were sold for only a couple of dollars.

The following year, the building was rebuilt in the same location and wooden decoy production resumed. However, Winterton started to develop health problems and scaled back on production and the number of employees. On August 14, 1952, he sold the building to the Pavco Veneer Mill and relocated his business to 425 North Magnolia Street on the Pascagoula River. The company produced only the decoys at this location, while the office and paint building remained on Pascagoula Street.

A pair of mint condition standard-grade bluebills by the Pascagoula Decoy Company.

A pair of PADCO standard-grade pintails.

127

Winterton's health continued to deteriorate, so on April 1, 1957, he sold the business to his longtime general manager, Adie Pittman. Pittman had been employed with Winterton for the past fifteen years and thoroughly knew the decoy business. Her husband, Dail, and son, Eddie Barton, also worked in the factory. Dail was employed by Ingalls Shipbuilding and worked part-time in the decoy plant. At an early age, Eddie attached the wooden decoy heads to the bodies, installed the eyes, and did some painting.

The Pascagoula Decoy Company continued manufacturing wooden decoys until 1959. The harvesting and transporting that was required made the gum and pop ash woods very expensive compared to the plastic and Styrofoam used by competitors. As a result, Adie Pittman decided to replace wooden decoy production with Styrofoam. According to her younger sister, Lucy Slade, who was employed as a decoy painter for the company for five years, Pittman wanted to signify the change and create her own identity by changing the name to the Singing River Decoy Company in 1960. They were the second decoy outfit in Pascagoula to operate under this name, with the Poitevin Brothers being the first.

The business was relocated back to North Pascagoula Street in a smaller building across the street from the Pavco Veneer Mill. The move was made primarily because the Magnolia Street location was prone to flooding on extreme high tides and during storms. Since the company no longer manufactured wooden duck decoys, there was no need for a large

A PADCO special-grade drake canvasback.

A rig of hen mallards once used by Robert Hanning, a local hunter on the Pascagoula River in the 1950s. Note the flat, "beaver-type" tail design that was common with their puddle ducks. This is a distinguishing feature of PADCO decoys.

facility to house and operate the lathes and other machines, and the new location was closer to Pittman's home. The Singing River Decoy Company offered Styrofoam decoys and sold them under the brand name "Singing River Decoys, Pascagoula, Miss.," which was printed on the bottom of the decoy. The company also sold fishing supplies such as paddles, oars, and tackle boxes and bait such as live crickets, minnows, and red worms. The company continued operation for eleven years and closed in 1971.

The wooden decoy production era ended for the Pascagoula Decoy Company with the plant closure at the Magnolia Street location in 1959. The wood products and decoys many hunters had grown up with merely became a chapter in the history of another Pascagoula industry. The Pascagoula Decoy Company was one of the last operations to produce wooden waterfowl decoys in the country and it played an important part in this rich history. Winterton's vision stayed in business for nearly twenty years, and his decoys received nationwide acceptance and became some of the best-selling decoys of the era. On July 16, 1963, Lester C. Winterton died at Baptist Hospital in New Orleans after a lengthy fight with cancer.

Top-flight-grade drake mallard in mint condition.

Supreme-grade drake bluebill.

Standard-grade drake canvasback.

Supreme-grade drake redhead.

131

Special-grade drake canvasback with worn but original paint.

Supreme-grade hen pintail. This model was hand-sanded for a smooth finish after leaving the lathe machine.

A rare PADCO baldpate or widgeon decoy in mint condition. Widgeons are the rarest of all species to find.

A pair of standard-grade canvasbacks in original condition.

Standard-grade redhead.

A pair of standard-grade pintails.

134

A rare PADCO drake goldeneye decoy in mint condition. Note the teardrop body shape that was characteristic of PADCO divers.

Black duck in mint condition. Both the hen and the drake were identical in appearance.

A salesman sample mallard decoy next to the company's top-flight model.

A salesman sample pintail decoy and the original.

A salesman sample pintail decoy made as an ashtray circa 1940s. These miniatures served as promotional items and toys.

A pair of supreme-grade mallards with the smooth finish.

137

Supreme-grade drake canvasback.

Supreme-grade drake scaup.

138

Pairs of supreme-grade mallards, pintails, and bluebills in mint, original condition.

The Pascagoula Decoy Company displaying their product line at a chamber of commerce event in Pascagoula, circa 1950s.

Adie Pittman inspecting the finished product before shipment. She was the general manager of the Pascagoula Decoy Company before purchasing the business from Lester C. Winterton in 1957.

A Pascagoula Decoy Company employee operating a band saw, separating two heads simultaneously produced on the lathe machine.

Decoys drying after being dipped in a gray primer. Afterwards, a final coat of paint was applied.

Quality paddles were produced for the navy, coast guard, and later the general public.

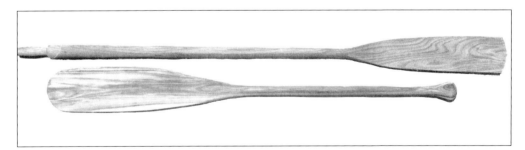

Varnished oars manufactured by the Pascagoula Decoy Company.

Ad from Outdoor Life Magazine, *June 1943.*

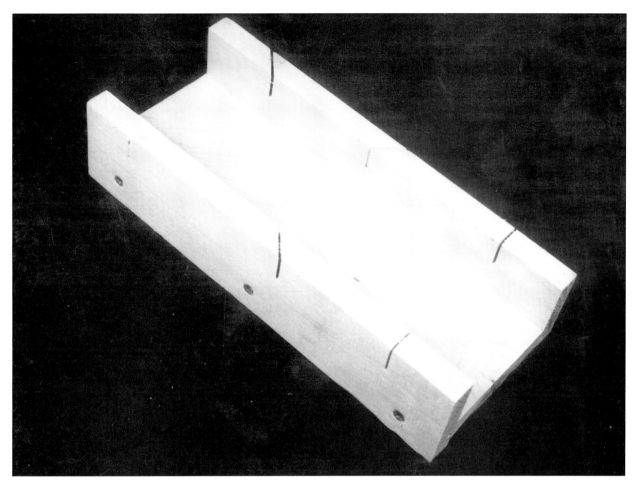

A miter box, one of the many different wooden products produced by the Pascagoula Decoy Company.

Ad from Outdoors Magazine, *November 1941.*

Styrofoam hen bluebill. These were made after the Pascagoula Decoy Company changed its name in 1960. The Singing River Decoy Company never produced wooden duck decoys.

Styrofoam drake mallard by the Singing River Decoy Company circa 1960s.

PASCAGOULA DECOY COMPANY

PINTAIL

A COMPLETE DECOY LINE

The well known PADCO line of wooden DUCK DECOYS includes four popular grades: "Supreme", "Top Flight", "Standard" and "Special". Each grade is available in nine species: Mallard, Pintail, Black Duck, Scaup (or Blue Bill), Ring Neck or (Black Jack), Canvasback, Redhead, Bald Pate and Golden Eye.

MATERIALS AND WORKMANSHIP

All of our Decoys are made of Tupelo Gum and Pop Ash, those famous cork-like woods from the swamps of the "Singing River." Each Decoy is carefully shaped to insure proper appearance and good "riding" qualities; the heads are trimmed and shaped by hand, and attached by means of a hardwood dowel and waterproof glue. Only the best paints, especially manufactured for the purpose are used. and all grades are hand painted.

SIZES AND WEIGHTS

The bodies of the Mallards and other large species are approximately 5½ inches wide. 12½ inches long and 3¼ inches thick; and their average net weight per dozen in the various grades are approximately: Supreme 18 lbs.; Top Flight 20 lbs.; Standard 23 lbs.; Special 25 lbs.

PACKING

Our standard packages of Decoys contain two-thirds drakes and one-third hens, packed in cartons of 6 or 12; and sample cartons of two— a drake and hen of one species. Special packs in other proportions can be made up at an extra charge of $1.00 per dozen, but additional time is required for their preparations.

Manufacturers of

PASCAGOULA DECOY COMPANY

BLUE BILL

PRICES

All prices are f.o.b. Pascagoula, Mississippi. and are subject to change without notice.

SALES TO INDIVIDUALS

While we sell primarily through jobbers and dealers, orders will be filled for individuals who are unable to purchase PADCO Products from their local store; but they are requested to furnish us their dealer's name.

TERMS

Sales to individuals are made on a strictly cash basis. and unless orders are accompanied by remittance, shipments will be made C. O. D.

DISCOUNTS

To Dealers who purchase for re-sale, and to Hunting Clubs who purchase in substantial quantities for club use, we are prepared to offer attractive discounts upon requests. and solicit their inquiries.

"SUPREME"

Our "Supreme" grade Decoys are made of the very finest and lightest Tupelo and Pop Ash obtainable. The bodies, heads and bills are hand finished and smoothly sanded; after which they are hand painted in natural colors and patterns, with special dull-finish paint. Truly a "Supreme" Decoy, exceptionally light in weight.

Size Pkg.	Shipping Wt.	Price
1 Doz.	about 20 Lbs.	$24.00
1/2 Doz.	about 11 Lbs.	12.25
1/6 Doz.	about 4 Lbs.	4.25

PADCO Products

1946 Pascagoula Decoy Company products catalog.

PASCAGOULA DECOY COMPANY

MALLARD

"TOP FLIGHT"

Made of selected, lightweight Tupelo and Pop Ash, with surface finished slightly rough to produce that "feathered effect" preferred by many hunters, and hand painted in natural colors and patterns—to "pull the high flyers in." An extra quality, light-weight Decoy—and our most popular grade.

Size Pkg.	Shipping Wt.	Price
1 Doz.	about 22 lbs.	$18.00
1/2 Doz.	about 12 Lbs.	9.25
1/6 Doz.	about 4 Lbs.	3.25

"STANDARD"

Made of choice Tupelo and Pop Ash and shaped to the same patterns as our higher grades; with the same slightly-rough surface as the Top Flights and hand painted in natural colors, but with somewhat less detail; these decoys are a quality product at a very moderate price.

Size Pkg.	Shipping Wt.	Price
1 Doz.	about 25 Lbs.	$15.00
1/2 Doz.	about 13 Lbs.,	7.75
1/6 Doz.	about 5 Lbs.	2.75

"SPECIAL"

Made of Tupelo and Pop Ash but generally of heavier weight, this grade consists primarily of "seconds" culled out of the better grades because of overweight, slight blemishes and minor defects. Good, serviceable Decoys, made on the same body patterns as the high grades, our "Specials" are a real "buy". But orders are accepted only subject to available supply.

Size Pkg.	Shipping Wt.	Price
1 Doz.	about 27 Lbs.	$11.00
1/2 Doz.	about 14 Lbs.	5.75
1/6 Doz.	about 6 Lbs.	2.25

Manufacturers of

PASCAGOULA, MISSISSIPPI

BLACK DUCK

NOVELTIES AND TOYS

In addition to our regular line of Decoys, we also make Miniature Decoys, suitable for use on the desk as paper weights—and most attractive for the den or mantlepiece. Being exact replicas of our regular decoys, these little miniatures (which are only about 2½ inches wide and 6 inches long) appeal to youngsters and grown-ups alike, and everyone who sees one wants it.

Among Toy Ducks, our "Waddie the Waddler" is in a class by itself. These fascinating toys are made from our regular sized decoys, which are so mounted on eccentric wheels that, when drawn across the floor by the attached pull-string, they imitate the waddling motion of a live duck in a most realistic manner (a feature protected by pending patent.)

PINTAIL AND MALLARD MINIATURES

MINATURES

Miniature Decoys—replicas of our Top Flights, but reproduced at ½ scale, these attractive little ornaments for the desk, mantlepiece or den are made in Mallard, Black Duck and Pintail Drake patterns only. Weight about 4 oz. each. Will not be available before late 1946.

Size Pkg.	Shipping Wt.	Price
1 Doz.	about 5 Lbs.	$15.00
1/6 Doz.	about 1 Lb.	2.75

PADCO Products

1946 Pascagoula Decoy Company products catalog.

PASCAGOULA DECOY COMPANY

PINTAIL

TOY DUCKS

"Waddie the Waddler"— the Toy Decoy that "waddles like a duck". A favorite with the kiddies—and often their parents, too. Available in Mallard Drakes only—except on special orders for large amounts.

Size Pkg.	Shipping Wt.	Price
1 Doz.	about 30 Lbs.	$15.00
1/2 Doz.	about 16 Lbs.	8.50
1/6 Doz.	about 6 Lbs.	3.00
1 only	about 3 Lbs.	1.75

BOAT OR CANOE PADDLES

During the war years we made hundreds of thousands of Paddles and Boat Oars for the armed services. We are now manufacturing them for civilian use, and can supply both in a variety of good woods and in a wide range of lengths. Paddles made of Cypress, Spruce, Ash. Maple and Oak are available in 5 ft. length, in addition to which Cypress and Ash Paddles are usually available in all lengths from 3½ ft. to 5½ ft.

Grades: Usually available in two grades (No. 1 and No. 2), the No. 1 Paddles are made of the choicest woods, while No. 2's may contain blemishes, discolorations, slight cross-grain, or small sound knots which would not be permitted in the better grade—so long as such defects do not materially impair their strength.

FINISH: All paddles are smoothly sanded and the No. 1's are finished with two (2) coats of clear Spar Varnish or waterproof enamel, while the No. 2's are usually finished with one (1) coat.

Manufacturers of

PASCAGOULA DECOY COMPANY

PRICES—Varnished

Lengths in Feet	CYPRESS & SPRUCE No. 1	No. 2	MAPLE & ASH No. 1	No. 2	CHERRY & OAK No. 1	No. 2
5	$2.50	$2.20	$2.30	$2.00	$2.20	$1.90

Lengths	CYPRESS No. 1	No. 2	ASH No. 1	No. 2
3½	$2.25	$1.95	$2.05	$1.75
4	2.30	2.00	2.10	1.80
4½	2.40	2.10	2.20	1.90
5	2.50	2.20	2.30	2.00
5½	2.70	2.35	2.50	2.20

BOAT OARS

Made of selected Ash, Maple. Cherry and Douglas Fir, and nicely finished by the most modern methods in smoothly sanded natural finish. our Oars are available in lengths from 5 to 18 feet.

PRICES PER PAIR

Lengths in Feet	ASH & FIR No. 1	No. 2	MAPLE & CHERRY No. 1	No. 2
5	$4.20	$3.90	$4.00	$3.70
5½	4.60	4.25	4.40	4.05
6	5.00	4.65	4.80	4.45
6½	5.40	5.00	5.20	4.80
7	5.80	5.40	5.60	5.20
7½	6.20	5.75	6.00	5.55
8	6.60	6.10	6.40	5.90
9	7.50	6.95	7.20	6.65
10	8.40	7.80	8.00	7.40

(Prices on longer lengths on request)

DISTRIBUTED BY

PADCO Products

147

PASCAGOULA DECOY COMPANY
Manufacturers and Distributors

Paddles   SPORTING GOODS ~ WOOD SPECIALTIES   Decoys
Boat Oars   STAPLE WOOD PRODUCTS   Duck Boats

P. O. Box 711 · Telephone 675

PASCAGOULA, MISSISSIPPI

1947 ~ DEALER'S Boat Oar and Paddle Price List ~ 1947

The following prices are f.o.b. Pascagoula, effective January 1, 1947. (Subject to
change without notice.)

PADCO Varnished Canoe Paddles

Length in Feet	Spruce & Cypress No. 1's	No. 2's	Maple, Ash & Beech No. 1's	No. 2's	Oak, Cherry & Poplar No. 1's	No. 2's
2-1/2	$1.40	$1.20	$1.20	$1.05		
3	1.50	1.30	1.30	1.10		
3-1/2	1.60	1.40	1.40	1.15		
4	1.70	1.45	1.45	1.20		
4-1/2	1.75	1.50	1.50	1.25		
5(*)	1.80	1.55	1.55	1.30	$1.30	$1.10
5-1/2	2.00	1.75	1.60	1.35		

ENAMELED Paddles ~ 5 Ft. Only in Green, Blue or Olive.

	No. 1's	No. 2's
Assorted Spruce & Cypress	$1.30	$1.15
Assorted Hardwoods	1.20	1.05

Paddles packed 25 per carton. Minimum order at above prices: 25 Paddles.
(*) 5' paddles can be shipped promptly, from stock at Pascagoula.

PADCO Boat Oars ~ Prices per Lineal Foot

Length in Feet	Ash & Douglas Fir No. 1's	No. 2's	Assorted Hardwoods (**) No. 1's	No. 2's
5 to 7-1/2	$0.33	$0.32	$0.33	$0.30
8 and 9	.36	.33	.34	.31
10	.38	.35	.35	.32
11	.42	.38	.39	.35
12	.45	.41	.42	.38
13	.50	.44	.45	.40
14	.55	.48	.50	.44
15	.61	.52	.56	.49
16	.67	.57	.62	.54
17	.72	.63	.67	.58
18	.77	.68	.72	.63

Oar prices are f.o.b. Pascagoula or factory in Pennsylvania. Minimum order at above
prices: Two Dozen (24) Oars.

Terms: 2% ~ 10 days, net 30 ~ subject to approval of credit. Until credit has been
approved (or if account is in arrears) shipments will be made only C.O.D. unless paid
for in advance.

(**) The assorted hardwoods consist principally of Maple, Cherry and Oak.

1947 Pascagoula Decoy Company oar and paddle price list.

1947 Pascagoula Decoy Company short paddles price list.

PASCAGOULA DECOY COMPANY
Manufacturers and Distributors

Paddles   SPORTING GOODS ~ WOOD SPECIALTIES   Decoys
Boat Oars   STAPLE WOOD PRODUCTS   Duck Boats

P. O. Box 711 · Telephone 675

PASCAGOULA, MISSISSIPPI

February 1, 1947

SPECIAL TO DEALERS ~ Short Paddles

Supplementing our regular line of Paddles, we also have moderate quantities
of reconditioned Paddles in 2-1/2, 3 and 3-1/2' lengths.

These are made by cutting back longer paddles that have been culled out due
to short splits in the ends of the blades, or because of defects in the
handles. They are made serviceable by trimming back the ends of the blades,
cutting out a section of the handle, and then rejoining the handle by means
of a hardwood dowel and Weldwood glue.

While they are not to be confused with either our regular No. 1 or No. 2
grade Paddles, we have only received reports of 5 or 6 cases where they have
failed at the joint ~ out of several thousand shipped in 1946.

These "reworked" Paddles are available in assorted softwoods (Spruce and
Cypress), or in assorted hardwoods, either varnished or enameled green or
O.D., at the following prices:

Type Wood	Varnished	Enameled
Softwoods	$1.20	$1.10
Hardwoods	1.10	.95

We can also furnish at a special price, moderate quantities of Paddles 4'-9"
long. These, too, have been recovered from 5' culls by trimming off split
blade tips. They are identical with our regular 5' Paddles except as to
blade length and are priced as follows:

Type Wood	Varnished No. 1's	No. 2's	Enameled
Spruce & Cypress	$1.50	$1.40	$1.25
Maple, Ash & Beech	1.30	1.20	1.15
Oak, Cherry & Poplar	1.20	1.10	1.05

All Paddles packed 25 per carton.

All prices f.o.b. Pascagoula and subject to change without notice.

PASCAGOULA DECOY COMPANY
— Manufacturers and Distributors —

Paddles
Boat Oars

SPORTING GOODS — WOOD SPECIALTIES
STAPLE WOOD PRODUCTS

Decoys
Duck Boats

P. O. Box 711 · Telephone 675

PASCAGOULA, MISSISSIPPI

1947 — DEALER'S DECOY PRICE LIST — 1947

Our popular "PADCO" line of DEPENDABLE Tupelo wood DUCK DECOYS is now available in our four well known grades: SUPREME, TOP-FLIGHT, STANDARD and SPECIAL.

In nine species — Mallard, Pintail, Blue Bill, Black Duck, Canvasback, Bald Pate, Ring Neck, Golden Eye and Redhead; packed two-thirds drakes and one-third hens of one species, in cartons containing 6 or 12 decoys each.

The following Dealer's prices are net Per Dozen, in cartons of 12 (see note 1 below), f.o.b. Pascagoula, Mississippi.

GRADE	DESCRIPTION	LIST PRICE	DEALER'S PRICE
SUPREME	(Extra light, smooth finish)	$24.00	$16.00
TOP-FLIGHT	(Extra light, rough finish)	18.00	12.00
STANDARD	(Regular weight, rough finish)	15.00	10.00
SPECIAL	(Seconds — see note 2 below)	11.00	7.50

Sample Carton of 6 in assorted grades and species .... $ 6.50

Note 1: For shipment in cartons of 6, add 25c per dozen to above prices.

Note 2: Our "Special" Brand is made up of decoys which have been culled out of the better grades, due to over-weight, or to minor defects. But they are all good, serviceable decoys. Orders for this grade, however, can be accepted only subject to available supply.

Terms: Our regular terms are 2% — 10 days, net 30 days. However, where customer regularly pays on the 10th of month following date of invoice, a discount of 1% will be allowed. New customers (unless listed by Dun and Bradstreet) are requested to submit credit references with first order, as all shipments will be made C.O.D. or B-L attached unless credit has been established.

ASSOCIATE MEMBER NATIONAL SPORTING GOODS ASSOCIATION

1947 Pascagoula Decoy Company dealer's decoy price list.

PASCAGOULA DECOY COMPANY
Manufacturers of Wood Sporting Goods
P. O. Box 711
PASCAGOULA, MISSISSIPPI

January 12, 1955

WHOLESALE MITRE BOX PRICE LIST

PADCO Wooden Mitre Boxes are made of selected Kiln Dried Hardwoods (Beech, Oak and Ash). The bottom and sides are 3/4" thick and are joined with tongued and grooved joints to prevent any possible slippage.

One side projects 1/4" below the bottom, for holding against work bench, and both sides are securely attached to the bottom by means of wood screws.

Type "W" and Type "S" Mitre Boxes differ in their fastenings, in that the sides of Type "W" boxes are secured to the bottom with four (4) wooden dowels, in addition to the wood screws. Both types are slotted for cutting 45° mitres right and left as well as for cutting 90° cut-offs, and are available in three grades: "A", "B" and "seconds".

Both types are made in the following dimensions (inside measurements): Length 16", Depth 1-5/8"; in addition to which Type "S" is also available in 12" length.

Packed either 1/2 Dozen or 3 Dozen per carton, shipping weights are as follows:

16" Mitre Boxes,	35 Lbs. Per Doz.	390 Lbs. Per Gross
12" Mitre Boxes,	28 Lbs. Per Doz.	295 Lbs. Per Gross

DEALER'S NET PRICES, f.o.b. Pascagoula, Mississippi, are as follows:

Type	Length	Grade "A" Dozen	Grade "A" Gross	Grade "B" Dozen	Grade "B" Gross	"Seconds" Dozen	"Seconds" Gross
"W"	16	$13.80	$162.00	$10.50	$121.50	$7.75	$89.10
"S"	16	12.60	147.50	9.50	110.50	7.10	81.25
"S"	12	10.45	121.50	7.85	91.10	5.90	66.80

GRADES: Grade "A" Boxes are free of noticeable defects. Grade "B" Boxes have minor defects and blemishes, but are of good general appearance. The "Seconds" admit more pronounced defects, both in wood and millwork – but none which would impair their serviceability.

DELIVERIES: While we are generally able to make prompt shipment, there are times when our stock of certain numbers is exhausted. Therefore, if time of delivery is important, it is advisable to indicate if any substitution would be acceptable, either in Type or Grade.

TERMS: 2% 10 Days; Net 30 (subject to approval of credit); otherwise 25% with order, balance C.O.D. All prices subject to change without notice – ALSO Guaranteed Against Decline for 90 Days!

JOBBER'S DISCOUNT: 20% off of the above prices.

1955 Pascagoula Decoy Company wholesale miter box price list.

PASCAGOULA DECOY COMPANY
Manufacturers of Wood Sporting Goods
P. O. Box 711
PASCAGOULA, MISSISSIPPI

January 12, 1955

1955 - WHOLESALE DECOY PRICE LIST - 1955

Our popular "PADCO" line of DEPENDABLE wooden Duck Decoys are available in our FOUR well known Grades: "Supreme", "Top Flight", "Standard" and "Special", and in ten species - Mallard, Pintail, Bluebill, Black Duck, Canvasback, Redhead, Ring-Neck, Baldpate, Golden Eye and Coot or poule-d'eau.

The following prices are Net, Per Dozen, f.o.b. Pascagoula, Mississippi, and the weights shown are approximate average shipping weights. Our standard pack consists of six drakes and six hens per carton. For special packs, such as all drakes or all hens, an additional charge of $1.00 per dozen will be made: and the scheduling and preparation of such special orders will usually require from two to three weeks additional time.

Grade	Weight	Description	Jobber	Dealer	Retail
SUPREME	18	Extra Light, Smooth Finish	$16.00	$20.00	$30.00
TOP FLIGHT	20	Extra Light, Rough Finish	12.50	18.00	24.00
STANDARD	22	Regular Weight, Rough Finish	10.00	12.50	19.00
SPECIAL	22	Good "Seconds" (See Note)	8.00	10.00	15.00

Note: Our "Special" Grade consists of Decoys culled out of the better grades, due to over-weight or minor blemishes, but are good, servicable Decoys. However, since we naturally never TRY to make "seconds" and the percentage that does develop is small, we never have a great many in stock. Consequently, orders for "Specials" can be accepted only subject to available supply.

PADCO Decoys have proven their superiorty for many years, from Coast to Coast. Because of their natural shape, lifelike colors and realistic action on the water, they are first choice of seasoned hunters - for their DEPENDABLE RESULTS!

Undercoated with Sealer for water-resistance and hand painted with high quality special "flat" colors to prevent gloss or reflection, they give years of service when given reasonable care. However, NO wooden Decoy (and very few others) should be considered completely "waterproof", and cannot be so guaranteed. They should be removed from the water after each hunt and permitted to dry until they are used again.

The success of most duck hunts depends far more upon the Decoys than upon the gun that is used. They should be treated accordingly - and cared for properly.

TERMS: 2% 10 Days, Net 30 (subject to approval of credit); otherwise 25% with order, balance C.O.D. All prices subject to change without notice - AND GUARANTEED AGAINST DECLINE for 90 Days!

Catalogue Pages Available on Request.

1955 Pascagoula Decoy Company wholesale decoy price list.

PASCAGOULA DECOY COMPANY
Manufacturers of Wood Sporting Goods
P. O. Box 711
PASCAGOULA, MISSISSIPPI

January 12, 1955

WHOLESALE SAW HANDLE PRICE LIST

We can make prompt shipment of Handles for regular size Hand Saws, Finishing Saws or Small Hand Saws, Compass Saws and the main Handles for 1-Man Crosscut Saws.

These Handles are made of selected Kiln Dried Beech, shaped to standard patterns, smoothly sanded and nicely finished. They are comparable in quality and appearance with handles made by the major saw companies and fit practically all standard make saws.

All handles except Compass are priced and shipped without bolt holes. (If bolt holes are desired, submit details of required boring for quotation). Packed 1 dozen per carton, 12 cartons per case, SHIPPING weights and DEALER'S NET PRICES, f.o.b. Pascagoula, are as follows:

TYPE HANDLES	Weights Doz.	Lbs. Gross	Grade "A" Doz.	Gross	Grade "B" Doz.	Gross	"Seconds" Doz.	Gross
Hand Saw, Carved	7-1/2	93	$8.35	$96.00	$7.15	$81.60	$5.50	$62.40
Hand Saw, Plain	7-1/2	93	7.85	90.00	6.70	76.50	5.15	58.00
Finish Saw, Carved	5	63	6.50	75.00	5.55	63.75	4.30	48.75
Finish Saw, Plain	5	63	6.20	71.50	5.30	61.00	4.10	46.25
Compass Saw, Carved	4	48	4.25	48.00	3.25	36.00	2.45	27.00
Compass Saw, Plain	4	48	4.00	45.00	3.00	33.60	2.30	25.20
1-Man Crosscut, Plain	7	90	6.35	72.00	5.35	60.00	3.90	43.20

JOBBER'S DISCOUNT: 25% off the above prices.

GRADES: Grade "A" Handles are free of defects and have a high gloss finish. Grade "B" have minor defects and blemishes, but are of excellent general appearance, with semi-gloss finish. The "Seconds" have more pronounced blemishes and defects, but are good servicable handles, with semi-gloss finish.

Deliveries of all types in Grade "A" can be made from stock or within a few weeks. Grade "B" and "Seconds" are available only as they develop. Where prompt shipment is essential orders should show acceptable substitutes as to grade and carving.

TERMS: 2% 10 Days; Net 30 (subject to approval of credit) otherwise C.O.D.

Prices subject to change without notice. GUARANTEED AGAINST DECLINE for 90 Days!

1955 Pascagoula Decoy Company saw handle price list.

P A S C A G O U L A   D E C O Y   C O M P A N Y
Manufacturers of Wood Sporting Goods
P. O. Box 711
PASCAGOULA, MISSISSIPPI
February 21, 1955

JOBBERS' NET PRICE LIST
VARNISHED CANOE PADDLES

Lengths In Feet	Spruce & Cypress		Oak, Ash, Maple & Cherry	
	No.1's	No.2's	No.1's	No.2's
2*	$0.75	$0.60		
5	1.50	1.15	$1.30	$1.00

* The 2' Paddles are available only in Cypress.

ENAMELED PADDLES

Lengths In Feet	Spruce & Cypress		
	No.1's	No.2's	(Green and O. D.)
4-3/4	$1.30	$1.05	
5	1.35	1.10	

Note: All Paddle prices are Each, and are based on standard pack
of 25 Paddles of one kind and length per carton. An extra charge
of 5% will apply on smaller lots or mixed cartons, to cover the
cost of opening cartons and repacking.

ASH BOAT OARS
(Oar Prices are Per Lineal Foot)

Lengths In Feet	Unpainted		Painted	
	No.1's	No.2's	Standard	Special
5 to 7-1/2	$0.27	$0.23	$0.23	$0.20
8	.29	.25	.25	.22
10	.33	.29	.29	.25
12	.40	.35	.35	.30
13	.45	.38	.38	.33
14	.47	.40	.40	.35
15	.52	.45	.45	.40
16	.55	.48	.48	.42
18	.65	.57	.57	.50

Oars up to 8' long are packed in cartons of 12; longer lengths are
bundled for shipment. If crating is required, add 3¢ per lin. ft..
For Fir oars, when available, deduct 20% from above prices.

BOAT HOOKS and POLES

	No.1's	No.2's
Bronze Boat Hooks with 12' x 1-1/2" poles	$2.25	$2.00
Same as above, except w/8' x 1-1/2" "	1.75	1.50
8' x 1-1/2" Ash Boat Poles, without hook,	0.65	0.50
12'x 1-1/2" Same " "	(Out of stock)	

Note: Boat Poles are unpainted. If painting desired, add 2¢ per Ft.
per coat. For varnishing add 3¢ per ft. per coat. Shipped bundled.

Terms: 2% 10 days; Net 30 - subject to approval of credit; otherwise
25% with order, balance C.O.D. Prices subject to change without notice.
All prices are f.o.b. Pascagoula, Mississippi or New Orleans, Louisiana.

1955 Pascagoula Decoy Company canoe paddles price list.

1955 Pascagoula Decoy Company products catalog, front cover.

PADCO *Duck* DECOYS

available in four grades
Packed ½ Drakes and ½ Hens

"SUPREME"
GRADE

Our "Supreme" grade Decoys are made of the very finest and lightest Tupelo and Pop Ash obtainable. The bodies, heads and bills are hand finished and smoothly sanded; after which they are hand painted in natural colors and patterns, with special dull-finish paint. Truly a "Supreme" Decoy, exceptionally light in weight.

Size Pkg.	Shipping Wt.	List Price
1 Doz.	about 18 Lbs.	▮▮▮ $30.00

"TOP FLIGHT"
GRADE

Made of selected, lightweight Tupelo and Pop Ash, with surface finished slightly rough to produce that "feathered effect" preferred by many hunters, and hand painted in natural colors and patterns — to "pull the high flyers in." An extra quality, light-weight Decoy.

Size Pkg.	Shipping Wt.	List Price
1 Doz.	about 21 Lbs.	▮▮▮ $24.00

"STANDARD"
GRADE

Made of choice Tupelo and Pop Ash and shaped to the same patterns as our higher grades; with the same slightly-rough surface as the Top Flights and hand painted in natural colors, but with somewhat less detail; these decoys are a quality product at a very moderate price.

Size Pkg.	Shipping Wt.	List Price
1 Doz.	about 24 Lbs.	▮▮▮ $19.00

"SPECIAL"
GRADE

Made of Tupelo and Pop Ash but sometimes of heavier weight, this grade consists primarily of "seconds" culled out of the better grades because of overweight, slight blemishes and minor defects. Good, serviceable Decoys, made on the same body patterns as the high grades, our "Specials" are a real "buy" But orders are accepted only subject to available supply.

Size Pkg.	Shipping Wt.	List Price
1 Doz.	about 25 Lbs.	▮▮▮ $15.00

Above list prices are subject to trade discounts to jobbers and dealers, who also may secure PADCO Duck DECOYS in assortments for sample or display purposes.

Orders from individuals who are unable to obtain PADCO Duck DECOYS from their dealers must be accompanied by full remittance and shipping charges will be C.O.D.

All prices are f.o.b. Pascagoula, Mississippi, and are subject to change without notice.

Write for FREE CATALOG of PADCO PADDLES AND OARS.

PASCAGOULA DECOY COMPANY
PASCAGOULA, MISSISSIPPI

Back cover.

PADCO *Duck* DECOYS *bring*

Designed by Duck Hunters!

PADCO Duck DECOYS are designed by duck hunters, to look like live ducks — **to real ducks.** It's what **ducks** think of your decoys that counts. PADCO Duck DECOYS have been "duck-tested" for years with remarkable "pulling" results.

Made of cork-like woods!

PADCO Duck DECOYS are made of kiln-dried Tupelo Gum and Pop Ash, the famous cork-like woods from the swamps of the "Singing River".

Shaped by wood-carving craftsmen!

Each PADCO Duck DECOY is expertly shaped to real-life appearance and correct proportions to assure realistic "riding" on the water. The heads are carefully carved and permanently attached by means of a hardwood dowel and waterproof glue.

Hand-painted by experts!

PADCO Duck DECOYS are impregnated with spar varnish for waterproofing, and then painted with the best grade flat paints especially manufactured for this purpose. Every decoy is hand painted to assure realism in color values and hues.

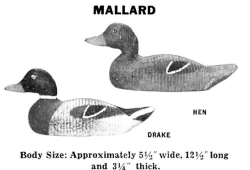

MALLARD

HEN

DRAKE

Body Size: Approximately 5½" wide, 12½" long and 3¼" thick.

Winter range: The entire United States, southern and western Canada, and Mexico.

PINTAIL

HEN

DRAKE

Body Size: Approximately 5½" wide, 12½" long (plus longer tail on Drakes) and 3¼" thick.

Winter range: Entire coastal areas of the United States, Mexico and Central America.

RED HEAD

DRAKE

HEN

Body Size: Approximately 5½" wide, 11" long and 3¼" thick.

Winter range: California, Mexico, and the Gulf Coast from Texas to Northwest Florida; and the Atlantic Coast from South Carolina to Massachusetts.

RING-NECK

HEN

DRAKE

Body Size: Approximately 5½" wide, 11" long and 3¼" thick.

Winter range: Southeastern United States.

SEE BACK PAGE FOR COMPLETE DETA

Interior spread.

154

g'em in!

Preferred by experienced duck hunters!

PADCO Duck DECOYS have been "duck-tested" for years by experienced duck hunters in every section of the nation. Experienced hunters who have "tried 'em all" prefer PADCO Duck DECOYS because they have proven the remarkable "pull" of these "duck-tested" decoys.

Built to last a lifetime!

PADCO Duck DECOYS are built to last a lifetime. They are made of solid cork-like wood, kiln-dried, impregnated with waterproofing Spar Varnish and painted with special high grade paint to assure years of satisfactory service.

Economically priced!

PADCO Duck DECOYS are made in four grades as described on the back page of this folder. Each grade is a real value in its class and the range of prices make it easy for every sportsman to own genuine PADCO Duck DECOYS.

BLACK DUCK

DRAKE AND
HEN ALIKE

Body Size: Approximately 5½" wide, 12½" long and 3¼" thick.

Winter range: From the lower Rio Grand Valley northeast to Maine.

BLUEBILL or SCAUP

HEN

DRAKE

Body Size: Approximately 5½" wide, 11" long and 3¼" thick.

Winter range: Entire coastal regions of the United States, Mexico and Central America, and the lower Mississippi valley.

CANVASBACK

HEN

DRAKE

Body Size: Approximately 5½" wide, 11" long and 3¼" thick.

Winter range: Coastal areas of entire United States (except lower Florida) and Mexico.

BALDPATE

HEN

DRAKE

Body Size: Approximately 5½" wide, 12½" long and 3¼" thick.

Winter range: Entire coastal areas of the United States, and Mexico.

GOLDEN-EYE

HEN

DRAKE

Body Size: Approximately 5½" wide, 11" long and 3¼" thick.

Winter range: The Pacific slope, the Mississippi valley and Eastern United States.

ILS, PRICES, PACKAGING INFORMATION

LUMBER
FOR SALE
Beautiful Flooring
Made of kiln dried Beech and Ash
Various Grades
Some Cypress and Pine 2x4, 2x6, and 8x8 framing, and boards suitable for trim. Also many short or narrow odds and ends.
PASCAGOULA
DECOY COMPANY
831 N. Pascagoula Street
22b 3 bc 1-2

Mississippi Chronicle-Star, *January 1948.*

22b BUILDERS' SUPPLIES 22b

Flooring!
Beautiful Kiln Dried 1 x 2 and 1 x 3 center matched Beech and Ash Flooring. New Low Price.
Pascagoula Decoy
Company
831 N. Pascagoula St.
22-b tf bc 1-13

February 1950.

COME BY AND SEE US FOR QUALITY RED WORMS AND CRICKETS. PADDLES, OARS, DECOYS AND FISHING TACKLE.
Singing River
Decoy Company
832 N. Pascagoula Street
Pascagoula, Mississippi
27 8tp 5-24

May 1960.

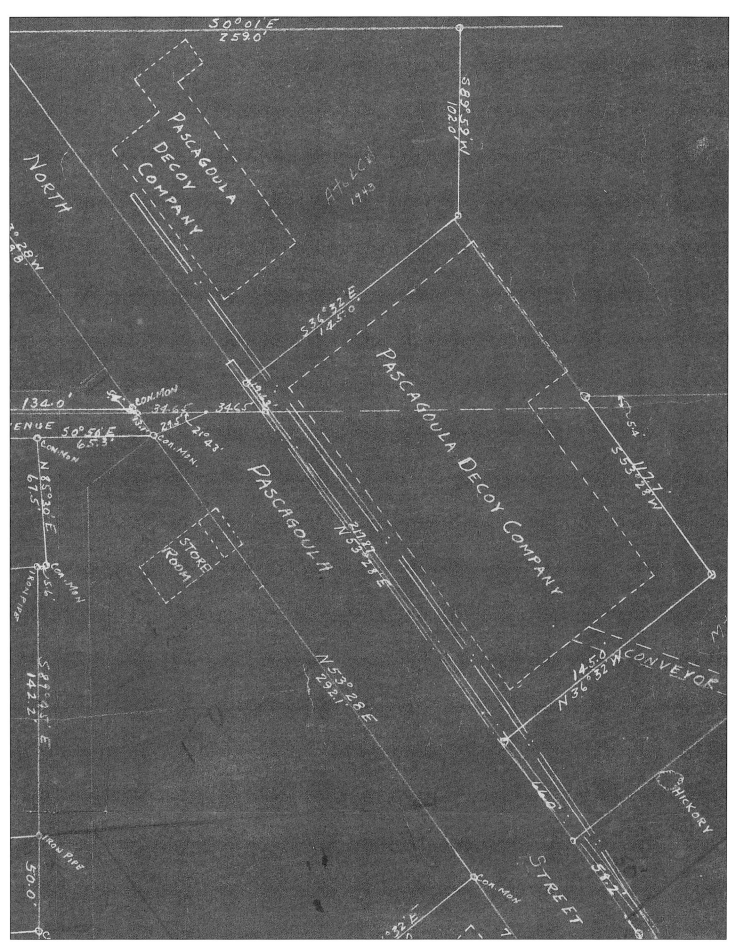

May 1944 layout of the Pascagoula Decoy Company plant on North Pascagoula Street.

SOURCES

American Factory Decoys, Henry Fleckenstein, Jr.
Animal Trap Company of America Employee Handbook
The Charles Ford Family Collection
Decoy Magazine, July/August 1994
Jackson County Archives and Library
Jackson County Business & Civic Guide
Jackson County Business Directory
Jackson County Business Review
Jackson County Chattel Deeds
Jackson County Tax Records
Mississippi Chronicle-Star
The O'Sullivan Family Collection
Pascagoula-Moss Point Advertiser

SUGGESTED READING

Barber, Joel. *Wild Fowl Decoys*. Dover Publications.

Decoy Magazine. P.O. Box 787, Lewes, Del. 19958.

Enger, Joe. *The Great Book of Wildfowl Decoys*.

Fleckenstein, Henry, Jr. *American Factory Decoys*. Schiffer Publishing, 1981.

——. *Decoys of the Mid Atlantic Region*. Schiffer Publishing.

Frank, Charles W., Jr. *Anatomy of a Waterfowl: For Carvers and Painters*. Pelican Publishing, 1982.

——. *Wetland Heritage: The Louisiana Duck Decoy*. Pelican Publishing, 1985.

Goldberger, Russ, and Alan Haid. *Mason Decoys*.

Haid, Alan G. *Decoys of the Mississippi Flyway*. Schiffer Publishing, 1981.

Luckey, Carl F. *Collecting Antique Bird Decoys and Duck Calls*. 1992.

McKinney, J. Evans. *Decoys of the Susquehanna Flats and Their Makers*.